Educational Interventions for Refugee Children

By focusing on the education of refugee children, this book takes a rare look at a subject of increasing significance in current educational spheres. Highlighting the many difficulties facing refugee children, the editors draw upon a wealth of international research and resources to present a broad, informative, and sensitive text.

The book identifies school-based interventions, whilst suggesting methods and measures with which to assess the efficacy of such programmes. It also develops a useful model that provides a standard for assessing refugee experience, offering diagnostic indicators for:

*   evaluating support services for refugee children;
*   future avenues of research;
*   practical implications of creating supportive educational environments for refugee children.

The need to identify and prepare for the education of refugee children is an international issue, and this is reflected in the broad outlook and appeal of this text. The editors have developed an overall model of refugee experience, integrating psychological, cultural and educational perspectives, which researchers, practitioners, and policy makers in education will find invaluable.

Dr Richard Hamilton and **Associate Professor Dennis Moore** are co-directors of the Research Centre for Interventions in Teaching and Learning at the University of Auckland.

Educational Interventions for Refugee Children

Theoretical perspectives and implementing best practice

Edited by
Richard Hamilton and Dennis Moore

RoutledgeFalmer
Taylor & Francis Group

LONDON AND NEW YORK

First published 2004 by RoutledgeFalmer
11 New Fetter Lane, London EC4P 4EE

Simultaneously published in the USA and Canada
by RoutledgeFalmer
29 West 35th Street, New York, NY 10001

RoutledgeFalmer is an imprint of the Taylor & Francis Group

© 2004 Richard Hamilton and Dennis Moore

Typeset in Sabon by GreenGate Publishing Services, Tonbridge, Kent
Printed and bound in Great Britain by TJ International Ltd, Padstow,
Cornwall

British Library Cataloguing in Publication Data
A catalogue record for this book is available from the British Library

Library of Congress Cataloging in Publication Data
A catalog record for this book has been requested

ISBN 0–415–30825–9 (pbk)
ISBN 0–415–30824–0 (hbk)

To the memory of my father, Gordon Hamilton

Contents

Illustrations

Figures

Tables

Contributors

Dr Angelika Anderson, Research Centre for Interventions Teaching and Learning, The University of Auckland

Kaaren Frater-Mathieson, M.Ed. (Hons), School of Education, The University of Auckland

Dr Richard Hamilton, Co-Director, Research Centre for Interventions Teaching and Learning, The University of Auckland

Dr Shawn Loewen, Lecturer, Department of Applied Language Studies and Linguistics, The University of Auckland

Associate Professor Dennis W. Moore, Co-Director, Research Centre for Interventions Teaching and Learning, The University of Auckland

Preface

The impetus for reviewing the literature on refugee education was a New Zealand Ministry of Education contract related to the evaluation of educational services to Kosova refugees entering the country in 1999–2000. The comprehensive review was focused on theory and research (both national and international) on the education of refugee children. We felt that while there was a large and diverse body of international literature around refugees addressing social, medical, political, linguistic and educational issues, there is a paucity of material specifically concerned with refugee children, and only a small proportion of this is about school-based interventions and programmes.

As we sifted through the research we started to see the possibility of deriving an overall model that would not only help in our evaluation of the specific Kosova refugee initiative but also other educational interventions for the education of refugees. In addition, we felt that we could contribute to the overall understanding of the plight of refugee children by integrating multiple diverse theoretical and research perspectives.

Within our initial literature review and in this expanded book, we have adopted an ecological model to impose some order on the wide array of contextual factors to be considered. Bronfenbrenner developed such a model, which illustrates the influence of the environment, or context, on child development. This perspective contrasts with others that could have been employed (for example, medical, psychiatric, psychological, sociological) and provides a useful and integrative conceptual frame in which to consider theory and research originating from these other perspectives. A review of this work has allowed the identification of what we believe are key indicators of both the resilience of the refugee child and his or her family and community, and the supportive qualities of the school system in which the refugee child is placed. Our intent in reviewing a broad array of research literature from a variety of disciplinary perspectives was to create a model which would apply across different refugee populations and host country education systems. Within the context of this ecological model, the intent of the book is to describe school-based interventions to help refugee children, to present a framework which integrates psychological, cultural and educational perspectives to assess the efficacy of such interventions, and to inform future best practice and research.

Acknowledgements

This book was born through an evaluation contract supported by the New Zealand Ministry of Education and we would like to thank them for their support of the literature review and their valuable suggestions and comments along the way. Clearly without this initial support and impetus, this book would not have come to fruition. However, I would also like to acknowledge that what developed and nurtured the literature review into the present edited volume was the spirit of collegiality shared by the contributors to this volume. We could see the value and the potential contribution that such a volume could make to the education of refugee children. Over never-ending meetings and discussions, we fine-tuned the model and ideas which we hoped would capture the complexity of the development and change of refugee children as they migrate and enter into a new educational environment. I would like to acknowledge, therefore, the importance and the value of collegial efforts as they help us shape our own individual ideas about education and its impact, as well as in shaping our collective ideas and those within the discipline of education.

I, Richard Hamilton, want to thank the rest of the Hamilton clan (Leslie, Megan and Marcus) for their endless support and for their penchant to make my life interesting and ever-changing.

I, Dennis Moore, want to thank my parents and family (Allen and Neila, Gail, Gareth, Caleb and Oliver), friends and colleagues (Angelika Anderson, Don Brown, Ted Glynn, Lottie Thomson, Joanne Walker) for their wisdom, good humour and support. A special thank you also to Richard Hamilton for his insightful and critical collaboration in this and other of our projects.

Chapter 1

Education of refugee children

Theoretical perspectives and best practice

Angelika Anderson, Richard Hamilton, Dennis Moore, Shawn Loewen and Kaaren Frater-Mathieson

Refugees are a legally and constitutionally well-defined group of people. While individual countries might have particular laws and regulations concerning refugees, there is an internationally agreed definition of 'refugee' contained in the Geneva Refugee Convention which was approved at a special United Nations conference held on 28 July 1951. This definition states that a refugee is

> A person who is outside his/her country of nationality or habitual residence; has a well-founded fear of persecution because of his/her race, religion, nationality, membership in a particular social group or political opinion; and is unable or unwilling to avail himself/herself of the protection of that country, or to return there for fear of persecution.
>
> (UNHCR 1993: 6)

According to the United Nations High Commissioner for Refugees, there are approximately 12 million refugees worldwide (UNHCR 2002). Children represent more than 50 per cent of these refugees, are among the most vulnerable of any refugee population and are often separated from their families as well as deprived of education. Refugee students are special because they have typically experienced both displacement and trauma and now face the task of adapting to a new environment, frequently involving the simultaneous acquisition of a new language.

With the world on the move in a way it has never been before, refugee children are becoming an identifiable and increasing group in today's schools. Refugee children share common refugee experiences of traumatic separation from their homeland and multiple experiences of loss, which contribute to a complex psychological, emotional, and social resettlement process. The effects of these experiences are further challenging for young people, who face these traumatic transitions into a new culture at critical times in their own psychological and social development. Thus, the struggle to preserve a sense of social and psychological stability at a time when there is a simultaneous need to acquire a new language and adapt to a new culture, places refugee children and young people potentially at risk of developing learning difficulties, behavioural problems and psychological distress. These populations of children, ranging from pre-school age through adolescents, represent groups potentially at risk for less than optimal outcomes at school.

Although some countries have experience in accommodating the special needs of refugee children, many education systems currently do not have special support systems in place to assist schools, refugee families and students in the process of adapting refugees to their new schools. It is crucial to know how to address their needs and how to create schools which are better prepared to meet their needs. To that end the aim of this book is to present a model for better understanding the psychological and educational needs of refugee children. In addition, the book will identify school-based approaches to help this population, and identify methods and measures to assess the efficacy of such interventions with a view to evaluating current practice and informing future 'best practice'.

Key issues identified in the literature

While there is a large and diverse body of literature on refugees that addresses social, medical, political, linguistic and educational issues, there is a paucity of material specifically concerned with refugee children; of this, only a small proportion is about school-based interventions and programmes. Much of the literature that is available focuses on culture-specific issues and effects, which the evidence suggests may not be generalizable across cultures (McCloskey and Southwick 1996). For example, cultural differences appear to exist in the interpretation of trauma, and in ways of coping. The same event, therefore, may have disparate effects on different groups of people and the same intervention may not be equally successful with all cultural groups. In addition, there are significant between-group differences that could affect outcomes, including the particular circumstances around the flight of the refugees, the time spent in refugee camps, and the cultural and geographical distance between the refugee group and the host country. Given this divergence of contributing factors and their potential effects, one of the purposes of this book is to provide a conceptual framework which can capture similarities in the changes in refugee children's learning and development across the different contexts and settings within which they live. With a more comprehensive framework for describing refugee experiences, we may be better positioned to use information from diverse refugee populations in forming general principles which guide the development and assessment of instructional interventions for all refugee children.

Bronfenbrenner contributed significantly to the field of developmental psychology by drawing attention to the importance of contexts in human development. His theory captures and illustrates the influence of the environment, or context, on child development (Bronfenbrenner 1999; Bronfenbrenner and Morris 1999). Given the diverse nature of refugees' experiences, the significance of contextual events past and present on refugee children and the need to impose some order on the wide array of contextual factors to be considered, we have adopted Bronfenbrenner's ecological theory of development as an integral part of our model. Bronfenbrenner's theory is outlined in more detail in the following section.

An ecological approach

According to Bronfenbrenner's ecological theory, development occurs in contexts, and can therefore only be properly understood in contexts (Brooks-Gunn 2001). In Bronfenbrenner's words, the essence of his theory is as follows:

> The ecology of human development is the scientific study of the progressive, mutual accommodation, throughout the life course, between an active, growing human being, and the changing properties of the immediate settings in which the developing person lives, as this process is affected by the relations between these settings and by the larger contexts in which the settings are embedded.
>
> (Bronfenbrenner 1992: 188)

Bronfenbrenner's model separates aspects of the environment according to the immediacy with which they impact on the developing child, namely the microsystem, mesosystem, exosystem and macrosystem.

First there is the microsystem, which, according to Bronfenbrenner's updated formulation, is:

> ... a pattern of activities, roles, and interpersonal relations experienced by the person in a face-to-face setting with particular physical and material features, and containing other persons with distinctive characteristics of temperament, personality and a system of belief.
>
> (Ibid.: 227)

The microsystem thus describes the relationship between the individual child and the immediate settings which impact on the child (family, neighbours, peers and so on).

In contrast, the next two aspects – the mesosystem and the exosystem – describe the relationship between the different settings which may impact the child. The mesosystem, which Bronfenbrenner refers to as a series of microsystems, describes relationships between proximal settings in which the individual is directly involved (for example, the relations between home and school, and school and work place). The exosystem describes the relationships between more distal systems, at least one of which the individual is not directly involved in (for example, for a child, the relation between the home and the parent's work place; for a parent, the relation between the school and the neighbourhood group).

Finally, the macrosystem constitutes the broad ideology, laws and customs of a society. It represents the consistencies evident in all the other settings within a society or culture, such as how all schools within one country share a number of features and are different in consistent ways from schools in other countries. The macrosystem is the overarching pattern of micro-, meso- and exosystems, which characterize a given culture, subculture, or broader social context. In particular it determines the belief systems, resources, hazards, lifestyles, opportunity structures, life course options, patterns of social interchange and so on, which influence development. The macrosystem may be thought of as a societal blueprint for a particular culture, subculture, or other broader social context (Bronfenbrenner 1992).

Bronfenbrenner visualized these interacting systems as nested one inside the other. Two important implications to be derived from his theory are first, that development is a process of mutual accommodation, characterized by reciprocity (that is, the person is not only influenced by his or her environment, but also influences that environment) and second, that the environment of interest is not a single, immediate setting, but incorporates several settings and the interconnections between them.

Bronfenbrenner's theory is thus a tool for describing human development which takes into account the role that environments play in the process. According to Bronfenbrenner, evidence that development has occurred requires not only an enduring change in the individual, but also a generalization of this change across settings.

Bronfenbrenner's theory provides a useful conceptual framework for considering the needs of refugee children as it allows us to consider the impact of personal and environmental factors on the development of refugee children. This is because at its core the theory conceptualizes development as the interactive life-long process of adaptation by an individual to the changing environment. For most individuals, environmental changes are gradual ones, or only affect some aspects of their lives, whereas refugees need to adapt to abrupt and major changes in almost all aspects of their lives. However, the processes by which this adaptation occurs are the same. Finally, the ecological approach allows us to look at a variety of divergent refugee populations through the same lens and get a better understanding of how the different overlapping and interacting systems influence the refugee child's development.

Relevant theoretical perspectives and related research

Bronfenbrenner's ecological conceptual framework helps organize the different influences on refugee children's development. Within this framework, we can draw on several independent but related fields of research to enrich our description of how the process of migration influences refugees as well as how we can best support refugees during the migratory process. The research falls into five broad categories: mental health literature related to grief, loss and trauma; the literature on displacement, migration and acculturation; literature on needs of linguistic and cultural minorities; literature on resilience; and inclusive education and special needs literature.

From these diverse sources of literature, a number of areas of research have been identified, the most relevant of which are discussed in the following sections. We have selected these areas because they help us to identify similarities and differences in refugee experiences across the different refugee groups. In essence, they give us a rich set of constructs with which to describe the refugee experiences as well as helping in the assessment and development of different educational interventions. When these constructs are paired with the ecological theory of child development, it helps identify the areas where educational interventions are needed for refugee children and whom the interventions should involve (for example, teachers, peers, family, or service providers).

The mental health perspective

Several reviews describe the refugee experience in terms of trauma and loss (Beiser *et al.* 1995; Fox *et al.* 1994; Kaprielian-Churchill 1996). Others discuss the applicability of the post-traumatic stress disorder (PTSD) construct for refugees as a group and describe associated symptoms in children (McCloskey and Southwick 1996; Pfefferbaum 1997). Much of this body of literature is situated in clinical contexts, with a focus on therapeutic interventions for individuals following identification and diagnosis. Though this particular body of literature largely describes pre-migration stressors, it also considers the ongoing trauma of adaptation to a new environment, and the issues of grief and loss associated with displacement. It is a useful and necessary approach to consider as it provides methods of identifying, supporting, and treating individuals for whom the stresses exceed their personal or contextual resources to cope, and who need intensive individual therapy.

Migration and displacement

In contrast to the mental health perspective, theories concerning displacement and migration largely concern themselves with post-migration stressors. Generally speaking displacement involves three separate issues: the physical change of location, the need to acquire a different language and the issues of culture and minority status.

The theoretical model we will use when considering the first aspect of displacement is 'the psychology of place' (Fullilove 1996). Displacement here is conceptualized in terms of the loss of attachment to a physical place, and the additional stress placed on individuals by the increased demands that result from having to orient the self in an unfamiliar space.

There is a large and diverse literature dealing with the cultural and linguistic issues of displacement, and with issues concerning minority populations. Culture is important in a number of ways. Cultural origins will influence both the way refugees interpret events and their styles of coping; and hence are an important consideration for developing appropriate interventions. It is also important to consider the process of acculturation which refugees undergo. This is particularly relevant for the identification of refugees as potentially at risk for developing oppositional cultural identities (Ogbu 1995a, 1995b) or negative acculturation attitudes (Berry 1987, 1995) because of the involuntary nature of their migration. This body of literature leads to the identification of contextual factors (both pre- and post-migration) which might moderate the traumas and stresses experienced, and which impact on the process of adaptation and the efficacy of interventions; for example, the cultural (as well as geographical) distance between the refugees and the host nation. In addition, this literature can help identify interventions that ease the transition to a new place, facilitate integration and prevent the negative outcome of marginalization.

Resilience

Resilience is defined by Blechman as 'the survival of a stressor (or risk factor) and the avoidance of two or more adverse life outcomes to which the majority of normative survivors of this stressor succumb' (Blechman 2000: 92). Masten and Coatsworth put it more simply as 'how children overcome adversity to achieve good developmental outcomes' (Masten and Coatsworth 1998: 205). These definitions make it clear that the literature on resilience is potentially useful in describing the task faced by refugees. It provides constructs which facilitate the integration of the diverse issues and factors which play a part in that task, namely adapting to a new environment at a time of great stress. Further, with its focus on strengths, existing resources and successful outcomes, this literature helps identify the factors (both personal and contextual) which facilitate healthy adaptation, and thus it supports the development of useful interventions, particularly those which are school-based. The personal and contextual variables that are known risk or resilience factors, and which act as barriers to or facilitators of the process of healthy adaptation, are used in this book to identify important variables that need to be considered when evaluating the efficacy of interventions and identifying best practice.

An inclusive approach to education

An increasing awareness of the role of the environment in relation to behaviour and learning has led to a shift in thinking and practice in meeting the needs of students with special needs (Moore *et al.* 1999; Walker *et al.* 1999; Reynolds 1989, 1992; Reynolds *et al.* 1987; Stainback and Stainback 1990). This has implications for the whole approach towards education within nations, and hence policy and administrative structures within institutions and service organizations (including schools). Refugees as a population of students are a good example of the kinds of students who could find themselves 'at the margins' (that is, unlikely to have their needs met) in a system where provision of services is dependent on classification and labelling. In addition, the very process of identification and labelling may adversely affect the process of adaptation and acculturation these students face under already trying circumstances. Finally, it is important to note that some refugee populations may be 'marginalized', not because they are struggling, but because they are exceeding the levels of performance of the native students.

Model for the education of refugee children

Our goal in developing a model for the education of refugee children is to facilitate a comprehensive consideration of the wide range of relevant factors which extend across the different refugee groups. The areas of research and theoretical perspectives described in previous sections are integrated within this model. The model we have developed is a developmental one. It can be used to track and describe change over time. In addition, we can employ the model to help us conceptualize the process of adaptation (the task faced by refugees) by considering the array of individual and environmental factors that hinder or facilitate this process. It allows us to examine existing and implemented factors (personal and contextual) that operate during the process of adaptation. Finally, the model facilitates the consideration of relevant outcomes and processes. A key feature of the model is the distinction between pre-migration, trans-migration, and post-migration factors. Pre-migration factors include those characteristics and experiences of the refugees that occurred prior to leaving the home country. Trans-migration factors include those experiences that occurred in the transition from home to host country. This could be a short transition that includes the plane trip from home to host country or could involve years spent hiding or in refugee camps prior to moving to the host country. Finally, post-migration factors include those experiences that occur on arrival in the host country. These factors are described, at each point in time, in terms of Bronfenbrenner's theory, which places the individual in his or her social and ecological context.

Figure 1.1 depicts the integration of an ecological approach to a refugee child's development with the different phases of the refugee child's experience: pre-migration, trans-migration and post-migration. Within this model, we suggest that at each of the three phases there can be dramatic tensions that arise due to atypical conditions within the ecological systems which impact on the child. An 'atypical condition' within this context is anything that either does not support or which interferes with the normal development of the child. These can be passive at one extreme in the sense that there may be a total lack of services (for example, health and education) or there may be factors which more actively work to break down the normal functioning of the child and those around the child (for example, war, torture and deprivation). Refugee children carry their past experiences

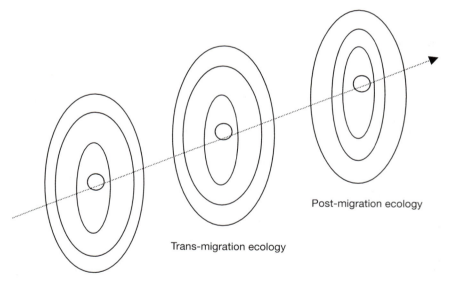

Post-migration ecology

Trans-migration ecology

Pre-migration ecology

Figure 1.1 **Model of refugee adaptation and development.** The development of the refugee child is influenced by the ever-changing ecologies that surround and interact with the child. For the refugee child, the potential for major changes in the nature of, as well as the presence or absence of systemic influences within, the ecologies can occur due to pre-migration, trans-migration and post-migration factors. These points of potential disruptions are in addition to the normal or typical points at which major developmental or ecological changes occur, e.g. entering into school, adolescence, and so on.

and expectations of their ecosystems, and their roles within those ecosystems, with them. They have to adjust to new ecosystem demands and relationships which occur as they go from the pre-migration to trans-migration to post-migration contexts. These differences in ecosystems are a function of the abnormal experiences which occur to refugees and of the fact that refugees most often move to countries which are quite different from their own. The major task for the refugee child and family, as well as for the schools and services within the host country, is to manage this transition as smoothly as possible, and establish some mutually beneficial and adaptive ecosystems. For the child and family the task involves adapting to the new environment, while the task for the school and services in the host country is to adapt and develop optimally supportive structures.

In summary, by using Bronfenbrenner's ecological theory of development we are able to capture snapshots of the different ecologies that refugees find themselves in at different points in time: pre-migration, trans-migration, and post-migration. These snapshots represent the kind of ecological and individual factors to consider at each point. In addition, there may be traumatic, stressful and disruptive events that affect the child's development. Most people experience a series of transitions in their lives; for example, the birth of a younger sibling, starting school, or moving house. Refugees as a group experience two major transitions that can have a profound impact on their lives: first, the flight from their home country, which in some cases is prolonged and characterized by extreme deprivation and traumatic experiences; and second, their arrival, at a time when their personal resources are low, in a host country which often differs radically from that to which they are accustomed. We are primarily concerned with factors that impact on the refugee child's ability to manage this transition into a new host country and, in particular, into a new school environment. However, all the experiences that precede the transition potentially influence this and need to be considered.

Our model helps identify the relevant factors and organizes them in two ways: first, at a point in time – pre-migration, trans-migration and post-migration – and secondly by utilizing Bronfenbrenner's ecological theory of development to identify individual, familial and broader ecological factors that influence the child's development across the three migratory phases.

Adaptation to a new school environment

As indicated earlier, one of the major tasks facing the refugee child when arriving in a new country is to adapt to a new school environment. Many of the refugee experiences, characteristics and circumstances, past and present, may have a significant impact on this process. Refugee children differ in what they bring to this situation including such factors as the degree of trauma experienced; how supportive the family is; and the child's and family's level of literacy in the first language. Likewise, there are a myriad of post-migration variables which will influence the child's ability to adapt to a new school environment. Some concern the individual child, others relate to the immediate and extended family and still others relate to the community, school and support services. The extent to which a child's family manages to adapt to its new surroundings and circumstances will impact on the extent to which the child can successfully adapt to the new school. In addition, unresolved emotional issues associated with displacement and trauma in the past can interfere with the child's ability to learn and develop within school. Also, the extent to which a subset of the familiar social environment has come with the child intact (family, extended family, friends and neighbours) will clearly impact the child's ability to thrive within school. Support services available in the host country, and the degree to which these are coordinated to help children and families, can either facilitate or present a barrier to the process of adaptation.

A third set of post-migration variables resides within the school; namely, the characteristics of schools and teachers. It is important to emphasize that adaptation is a mutual process. Not only will the child be required to adapt but schools, teachers and existing students will also need to adapt to the child. A critical characteristic of schools most likely to have positive effects on refugee children is a willingness to make changes for the benefit of refugee children. Consequently, any attempt to measure the success of any refugee educational intervention needs to focus not only on the individual child's adaptation as evidenced by changes in child behaviour, learning, peer relations and health, but also on the school's adaptation as evidenced by changes in school policies, procedures, practices and teacher development. Finally, there are developmental issues which concern the specific developmental tasks that 'typical' pre-school, primary and secondary school-aged students face in their lives; for example, the establishment and maintenance of peer relations and the development of independence.

Organization of this book

The following chapters have been organized to highlight the different aspects of the model outlined above. Bronfenbrenner's ecological model has been used to guide the writing of the individual chapters as well as to organize the sequence and relationship between chapters. Given the nature of our model and the adoption of an ecological perspective, there is overlap in the specific issues under consideration in each of the chapters.

Chapters 2 to 8 keep the individual refugee child as a focal point while discussing the influence of the progressively wider systems on the learning and development of the child. Chapter 2 concerns trauma, loss and grief. It centres on factors which directly influence the life and development of the refugee child, and considers what this means when placed in the context of educational settings.

Chapters 3 and 4 consider language and resilience respectively which, by their very nature, emphasize the relationship between individual children and their immediate environments. In particular, these chapters highlight the importance of taking advantage of existing literacy skills and coping strategies which can act as 'buffers' which may moderate the potential negative effects of migration and the refugee experience.

Chapter 5 focuses on children as members of communities (as migrants and cultural groups) and the struggles and processes connected with adaptation and acculturation, which occur at both group and individual levels. The inevitable clash between ethnic cultures as well as with institutionalized cultures (schools and families) is highlighted within this chapter.

Chapter 6 discusses how schools and teachers need to change and adapt in order to facilitate and support the education of refugee children. Both the changes required and the methods employed for implementing these changes are described. In addition, the importance of coordinating educational and therapeutic services is identified as a critical determinant of successful integration of refugee children within schools.

Chapter 7 looks at the broader context of refugee education and focuses on the interactions between schools (as representatives of society's mores and values) and other organizations, institutions and structures. This chapter addresses national policy issues and the impact of national educational philosophies in a multicultural society on the education of refugee children. Thus the chapters within the book move from a specific focus on the individual child, to the child's relationship with family and culture, to his or her integration within schools and, finally, to how national and societal issues can indirectly influence the refugee child.

Chapter 8, the final chapter, focuses on a description and summary of the diagnostic indicators for evaluating support services for refugee children, future avenues of research, and practical implications for creating supportive educational environments for refugee children. It summarizes the specific diagnostic indicators within the context of the model presented in Chapter 1 as well as identifying important future research directions. These indicators catalogue factors which may influence the pattern and success of the process of adaptation that each refugee child will engage in when entering into a new school and society. The chapter also summarizes best practice for facilitating the refugee child's development and learning within the school context. These issues are organized primarily along the lines used in the preceding chapters.

Chapter 2

Refugee trauma, loss and grief

Implications for intervention

Kaaren Frater-Mathieson

Traumatic events and traumatic loss overwhelm the ordinary human adaptation to life and the systems of care that give people a sense of control, connection and meaning (Herman 1992). For refugees it is the multiplicity of these losses and stressors of exile, in addition to traumatic events, that creates the complex situation which constitutes the refugee experience.

Migration in itself is both a challenging and a stressful experience. When this process co-exists with the often traumatic and violent pre-migration, trans-migration and post-migration experiences of refugees, the stress commonly surpasses an individual's or family's natural coping capacities.

On the whole, refugee children adjust and adapt to their new environment in the host country and are generally able to acculturate in the host society with more ease than adults (Ahearn and Athey 1991). Research nevertheless reflects that many refugee children are at increased risk for developing mental health problems (Stoehr 2001). Broadly speaking, for healthy psychological development, a child or adolescent needs three things: a sense of security, a supportive social network and opportunities to flourish and develop. However, with refugee young people, both traumatization and uprooting can interfere with their psychological development because they lack the necessary foundation of safety and security to achieve emotional, cognitive and behavioural competence. Learning, cognitive development and identity development may be delayed or complicated in refugee young people (Van der Veer 1998).

Of relevance here is Fullilove's concept of the 'psychology of place' (Fullilove 1996), which surmises that individuals endeavour to create a sense of belonging to a place. This need arises from three psychological processes: attachment, which is the bond between a person and a beloved place; familiarity, which is a person's knowledge and awareness of their environment; and identity, which pertains to the sense of self which develops out of one's intimate and immediate environment (ibid.).

For refugees, the experience of displacement is one of the most significant traumas and experiences of loss they face, and one which dismantles the emotional, spiritual and physical connections with place. Fullilove points out that the disorientation, nostalgia and alienation following such displacement may undermine the sense of belonging in particular, and mental health in general.

This chapter will focus on the dimensions and complexity of refugee trauma, loss and grief within the context of Bronfenbrenner's interacting ecological framework outlined in Chapter 1. It will review the theories and research on trauma, grief, loss and post-traumatic stress disorder in order to provide a better understanding of the effect of extreme experiences on the refugee child and adolescent and their coping responses throughout the three phases of pre-migration, trans-migration and post-migration. The chapter also considers the implications for best practice in the context of inclusive education, including issues of assessment, thereputic interventions and school, classroom and teacher practice.

Understanding trauma, loss and grief

It has been estimated that more than 10 million children in the past decade have suffered psychological trauma as a consequence of civil and international wars (Reichenberg and Friedman 1996). Despite this pervasiveness, however, there are many misinformed assumptions which limit the resources and support necessary for young people. These include the belief that they are too young to recognize what is going on around them, that young people will forget about the experience, that the effects are short-lived and that children are naturally resilient. Young people are resilient, but it is wrong to imagine they can recover without assistance from the cumulative trauma which characterizes the lives of many refugee children and adolescents (Kaplan 2000).

Not all young refugees will develop clinical symptoms as a result of trauma; however, every refugee child will have experienced some degree of trauma in relation to their experiences of disrupted family, school and community life, multiple losses and the effects of war, as well as with respect to the ongoing and complex family reunification and resettlement issues they face in the country of resettlement. The impact of these traumatic experiences on children and young people can, for some refugees, extend over a lifetime, with symptoms manifesting at particular developmental stages or significant events in an individual's life.

The measure and complexity of war and exile-related trauma and loss is enormous. Rando (1993) notes that trauma can have a number of mental health consequences, most notably post-traumatic stress reactions, anxiety, depression, helplessness and powerlessness, survivor guilt, and personality disturbances. Mourners are at particularly high risk for developing post-traumatic stress if, while being involved in the same traumatic event that took the life of loved ones, they feared for their own lives, felt powerless, and the event was shocking and unanticipated. Pre-existing vulnerability from earlier psychological wounding or trauma plays a part as well (ibid.).

It is critical, however, to avoid presupposing psychopathology if a disorder has developed after the trauma, unless there is clear evidence that such problems pre-existed and have influenced post-traumatic reactions over and above the normal response to trauma (ibid.). Clinical symptoms such as prolonged crying, fear, anxiety or other behavioural changes may initially be natural responses to experiences of overwhelming upheaval, loss and change. Clinical symptoms nevertheless need to be carefully and sensitively assessed, given that some symptoms such as dissociation can be maladaptive, leaving the individual more vulnerable to developing post-traumatic stress.

Psychological trauma is recognized as being influenced by both the actual exposure to an overwhelming experience and a process whereby the earlier coping strategies of the individual are rendered beyond their capacity to deal with the experience. There is consequently a loss of cognitive schemata, which normally allows the person to interpret life as a safe, organized and forseeable experience (Herman 1992; Montgomery 1998; Silove *et al.* 1991).

When an individual is exposed to a traumatic experience, the individual will often at first attempt to create meaning around the experience. Research on the effects of traumatic events on children have shown that children, too, will attempt to process and make sense of the traumatic experience, but their reactions are specific to their age, environment and their cognitive development (Corr and Corr 1996; Perry 1994).

As the child tries to make sense of what has occurred, the event will keep re-presenting in the child's mind. The child may reflect this by telling the story over and over again, acting out the event in play or using drawing to describe the traumatic event and intrusive recurring thoughts about the event. This re-living of the experience may also be manifested through intrusive dreams, which re-play the emotional or affective memory of the actual trauma (Perry 1994).

How an individual has previously adjusted and adapted to loss and other life challenges has significant bearing on the impact of trauma and loss. Researchers have identified several risk factors which make an individual more vulnerable to experiencing trauma symptoms. Pre-trauma factors are family dysfunction or parental inadequacy and prior experiences of trauma and traumatic loss. The nature and degree of the trauma are important variables, as are post-trauma risk factors such as loss of faith in self, adults and a supreme being, and inadequate support within the child's micro-systems. The nature of the family response to trauma experiences is also important (Corr and Corr 1996; Van der Veer 2000). Some children, for example, are indirectly affected by problems which stem from their parents' experiences with violence and persecution (Van der Veer 1998). If the parents are not adjusting successfully and impose their fears or burdens on the children, and there is no other interactive and mutually accommodating buffer of other support, children will also develop a sense that problems are overwhelming and that they are powerless in bringing about change.

The most notable symptoms reflected in children who have experienced significant trauma, directly or indirectly, are anxiety and fear. These changes may be manifested in various ways, such as an appetite disorder, stress-related physical ailments such as headaches or stomach aches, impulsive or regressive behaviour, hyperactivity, and mood changes from aggression to depression or withdrawal. There may be extreme reactions to mildly stressful events and an excessive physiological startle response, a refusal to go to their own bed, a fear of being alone, too much or too little sleep, and nightmares. There may also be some loss of previous functioning, or a slow rate of acquiring new developmental tasks (Kaplan 2000; Perry 1994). A research study of Central American refugee children in a school environment observed that exposure to war and persecution-related trauma resulted in significant delays in the children's academic and cognitive functioning above and beyond those that could be accounted for by a lack of proficiency in English (Ahearn and Athey 1991). Montgomery (1998) has also found in her emotional and behavioural studies of refugee children the occurrence of depression, aggressive behaviour and other emotional and behavioural symptoms .

Terr's (1991) study of traumatized children revealed that children's reactions to crises are varied, complex and profound. Nevertheless, familiar, cohesive patterns emerged in the studies. The descriptions were keyed to specific developmental stages. Terr found specific post-traumatic behaviours in pre-school children included withdrawal, denial, cognitive, emotional and relational thematic play, anxious attachment, specific fears and regression. In younger school-age children, the most common behaviours were performance decline, compensatory behaviour, obsessive talking, discrepancy in mood, behaviour changes or problems, more elaborate re-enactments and psychosomatic complaints. In older school-age children, some were likely to exhibit acting-out behaviours, display low self-esteem and be self-critical. Terr found that these school-age children sometimes developed joyless lifestyles several years in advance of their age, as well as displaced anger and a preoccupation with self .

A changing sense of self is also accelerated in bereaved children, who often talk about feeling older than their peers. However, bereavement, without accompanying trauma, has fewer debilitating and more constructive effects. It has been noted for example, that bereaved children can, in many instances, begin to value more intimate aspects of relationships and take themselves and their lives more seriously (Silverman 2000).

Healthy adjustments after specific traumatic experiences depend on cognitive competence, self-esteem, coping strategies, a stable emotional relationship with a parent or parental substitute and access to support from the former, in addition to access to a wide system of social support outside the family (Montgomery 1998). If, however, a child has been exposed to multiple prolonged traumatic experiences, the effects often have a greater impact on the child's emotional, moral and cognitive development, altering the individual's internal working model of the world and self.

A longitudinal study of resettled refugee children hypothesized that a child's age at the time of the traumatic events influences differences in symptomatic outcomes related to trauma. Those children who experienced the disruption of early, vital attachment relationships were more susceptible to developing oppositional or conduct traits at school than students who had roughly eight years of normal life prior to experiences of trauma, loss and exile (Ahearn and Athey 1991). This research has been qualified by other studies, which have observed younger children to be more at risk than older children if their relationship to their parents is affected through separation or deep seated trauma-related emotional responses in the parents. This research clarifies the significant influence of the microsystem on the child's response to trauma. If parents have successfully created a protective shield against the trauma and continue to maintain a secure relationship with their children, then younger children will not be as significantly affected as older children by the trauma and upheavals (Montgomery 1998).

The nature of post-traumatic stress disorder

It is necessary here to consider post-traumatic stress disorder (PTSD) in more detail. PTSD is the diagnosis given to a collection of distressing symptoms which can come into being after an individual has experienced, witnessed or been confronted with a terrifying and often life-threatening event or events, or has experienced, witnessed or been confronted with a threat to the physical safety or integrity of one's self or others.

Common PTSD indicators have been identified in four symptom clusters: affective indicators, physical indicators, cognitive distortions and behavioural indicators. Affective indicators include symptoms of pessimism, depression, anxiety, guilt, anger, grief and detachment. Physical indicators include nightmares, heightened arousal, somatic complaints, headaches, sleep disturbances and fatigue. Cognitive distortions include negative perceptions, intrusive re-experiencing of the trauma in some form, alternating with numbness, self-blame, loss of interest, impaired memory, suicidal ideation and poor concentration. Finally, the behavioural indicators include regressive behaviours such as clinginess, withdrawal, agitation, isolation, repetitive play and startled reactions (Cole 1996; Creamer 2000).

The diagnostic criteria for PTSD, as set down in the American Psychiatric Association's Diagnostic and Statistical Manual (DSM–IV), requires three sets of symptoms – namely, symptoms relating to re-experiencing the traumatic event, symptoms of avoidance and numbness in relation to the traumatic event, and persistent symptoms of arousal – to be present for at least a month, and for them to cause significant distress or functional impairment (APA 1994).

The PTSD field remains in its infancy in terms of rigorous empirical research, and considerable work needs to be done on theoretical models with the aim of developing an integrated bio-psychosocial model of PTSD (Creamer 2000).

Nonetheless, it can be a useful tool for understanding the psychological impact of the refugee experience (Friedman and Jaranson 1994). Several research studies on refugees reflect that PTSD symptoms are frequent after concrete war-related experiences (Montgomery 1998; Ahearn and Athey 1991). In a study of 81 refugees who were former political prisoners the researchers found a direct correlation between all PTSD measures and help-lessness, an overall feeling of alienation and a permanent change in personality (Ehlers *et al.* 2000).

However, notwithstanding its usefulness in assessing refugee responses to trauma, the diagnosis is regarded as culture bound, pure and rigorously defined, and not in tune with the multiple variables of the refugee experience (Friedman and Jaranson 1994; Montgomery 1998; Plummer 1998). Nor does it sufficiently recognize the more complex symptom picture of prolonged, repeated trauma (Herman 1993) which often characterizes the refugee experience. For example, the PTSD diagnosis does not give weight to ethnocultural, religious and socio-political contexts – or that coping with these related losses can produce a phenomenological picture that meets PTSD criteria, but which may instead be a process of cultural bereavement. (Eisenbruch 1991). In addition, the diagnosis does not take into consideration experiences of war, growing up in a camp or living with a traumatised parent – events that are characterized by the continuous presence and repetition of a number of different stressors, which together constitute a condition of influence (Montgomery 1998).

Montgomery (1998) proposes that specific traumatic events are best understood within a PTSD framework, but prolonged repetition of trauma is best understood in the context of developmental psychology. Hence, post-traumatic stress syndrome (PTSS) has been put forward as an alternative. PTSS offers a more general construct than the purely defined PTSD (Friedman and Jaranson 1994). PTSS overlaps with PTSD but it may also feature symptoms that are idiosyncratic to individuals from specific ethno-cultural traditions. It also recognizes that a profound, acute psychological response following traumatic exposure is universal. When, however, traumatic events are unable to be psychologically integrated by individuals, the psychological response can be transformed into a chronic and debilitating post-traumatic stress syndrome.

Herman (1993) has also developed a more varied and comprehensive concept of PTSD, which she termed Disorder of Extreme Stress not Otherwise Specified (DESNOS). This has also been called Complex PTSD. DESNOS or Complex PTSD includes in its symptom clusters and charac-terological features a broader spectrum of conditions, which can develop in response to prolonged and repeated trauma. This proposed concept of DESNOS/Complex PTSD calls attention to the characterological changes such as relationship disruption, repetition of harm, including self-harm and re-victimization, and changes in personality and identity.

Whether or not a diagnosis of PTSD is made, it is important to remember when working with young people who are refugees that the psychological effects are far more extensive than those captured by post-traumatic stress disorder. Loss that occurs under violent circumstances is known to lead to depression and profound grieving (Kaplan 2000).

Loss and grief

It has been noted that people work through grief not by abandoning it but by retrieving, consolidating and transforming the meaning of their relationship to the person they have lost (Rando 1993; Staudacher 1987). Neimeyer (1998) describes the anatomy of the grief cycle, particularly where the loss is sudden and unanticipated, as commonly moving through the three phases of avoidance, assimilation and accommodation – phases that are never even and can last for months, even years.

Avoidance is where the reality of the loss is impossible to comprehend, and the person grieving may respond initially with shock, numbness, panic or confusion. In the *assimilation* phase, the full impact of the loss is gradually absorbed and the person experiences intense loneliness and sorrow. Depressive symptoms are common during this phase, and there can be other physiological stresses too. *Accommodation* begins when the symptoms of grief lessen. This allows the individual to begin rebuilding the social world that has been shattered by the loss, not by replacing the loss or the one who has died, but by recruiting and strengthening a circle of relationships that are appropriate to the changed life to which one must now adapt (Neimeyer 1998).

This grief process is helpful in understanding the mourning of 'high grief' losses experienced by refugees. Nevertheless, for many young refugees the grief process can become problematic or more intense and prolonged, not only because they have lost a whole world of relationships but because ongoing grief for missing relatives can cause debilitating psychological distress.

Each survivor's grief is both similar to that of other refugee survivors and unique to the individual. It is helpful, however, to be aware of the factors that can influence significant psychological responses to loss. These include, for example, the suddenness of the loss, the number of traumatic losses the survivor experienced, the context and the specific circumstances in which they occurred and what each loss meant to the survivor. Secondly, experiences of multiple and traumatic loss are influenced by individual characteristics such as age, gender, personality, mental health and previous levels of coping and adjusting. Finally, there is the effect of cultural uprooting, which can result in the loss of self-identity, cultural values and traditions and meaningful social structures (Almqvist and Brandell-Forsberg 1997; Eisenbruch 1991).

For young people there are a number of secondary effects associated with traumatic and unresolved grief. Some common age-related effects associated with traumatic loss for the 6–12 year age group include difficulty with concentration; learning difficulties; conduct disturbances; re-enactments of loss; feelings of guilt; passivity and lack of spontaneity; aggressive and demanding behaviour; social isolation; headaches and stomach aches; and death anxiety.

Characteristics displayed by adolescents may include premature adoption of an adult role; premature identity formation or identity confusion; use of self-destructive behaviours to distract from sadness; acting out and antisocial acts; feelings of guilt; feelings of shame and isolation; pessimism about future; disturbances in self-image (Kaplan 2000).

Although it is important not to pathologize grieving, it is essential to recognize that satisfactory reorganization of one's life following traumatic and multiple loss is not a guaranteed outcome (Neimeyer 1998). This will invariably affect the young person's ability to concentrate and learn in the classroom environment. Thus extra social and professional support needs to be available in order to help a young person create a healthy balance between developing a symbolic connection with all that has been lost and, at the same time, readjusting and establishing other forms of connection to the changed world into which he or she has been thrown.

The preceding sections reviewed theories and research on trauma, grief, and post-traumatic stress disorder in order to help us better understand the effect of extreme experiences on the refugee child and adolescent, within the context of their ever-changing microsystems, mesosystems and exosystems. Given this as an underlying framework, the following sections will focus on pre-, trans- and post-migration factors which may influence a refugee child's development and learning.

Influence of pre-migration factors on children

Refugee children come from a diversity of cultures and experiences, and so cannot be placed systematically in the one category. Some children may have been exposed to extended violence and trauma in war zones and transition camps and have lost supportive family members. Other children may have escaped before being exposed to or witnessing war-related events. A child's age, culture, cognitive processes, emotional experiences and parental support are also variables which affect a young person's ability to cope with traumatic experiences and adjust to new stressful circumstances. Nevertheless, traumatic loss and change is a marked characteristic of all refugee children.

Common pre-migration experiences for refugee children are of living in a country where their family and the wider community experienced increased repression or political persecution over a number of years. This can include the loss of their home, their friends and, in many cases, their parents or siblings. A number of refugee children may also have witnessed the rape and execution of family members. The psychological ramifications of this can be both immediate and long-term (Ahearn and Athey 1991; Van der Veer 1998). When we look at the impact of such loss and change on the family, where often one or more individuals will have experienced trauma and in some cases torture, the already fragmented family system experiences further stress and disempowerment.

Torture, for example, is commonly interwoven in the socio-economic structure of a number of countries and consequently impacts on the society, family and individual. It is used as an apparatus in destroying not just individuals and families, but whole communities and cultures and thus preserving an oppressive system. In a recent study of Middle Eastern refugee families in Denmark, 51 per cent of the children were part of a family which included a survivor of torture (Montgomery 1998). As mentioned above, psychological torture impacts not only on the individual, but also the family and community. It induces self-denigration and a deep sense of loss – of relationships to family and community and consequent loss of trust, dignity, values, belonging, and self. For many survivors, torture is as an ongoing state they are unable to put in the past. Silove *et al.* (1991) note that the defences survivors often use to cope with torture, such as splitting, numbing, or projection, continue to be used in the resettlement process. This may lead to heightened communication difficulties and strong emotions, especially anger and irritability, which places further stress on a refugee family.

There can also be secondary losses such as the loss of a sense of safety, familiarity, confidence in one's self and others, identity, and well-being. There can be sudden changes in attachment figures and relationships and often the ability of the child's parent or caregiver to provide emotional and physical support is diminished.

As discussed earlier, research on refugee children has identified pre-school (Bowlby 1980) and early adolescence (Ahearn and Athey 1991) as the most vulnerable years for refugee children who experience pre-migration ordeals of war-related events. Because of their limited cognitive resources and consequent difficulties in comprehending and processing experiences, pre-school children are particularly sensitive to traumatic events (Montgomery 1998). This changes when children reach school age, because children then have more cognitive, emotional and behavioural resources for handling traumatic situations (ibid.). It has also been noted that although refugee pre-migration experiences occur at a time when children are more vulnerable in certain ways, they are also more adjustable and flexible when compared with refugee adults. These qualities are, however, dependent on the children's parents being in a position to support and protect them (Ahearn and Athey 1991).

Influence of trans-migration factors on children

Trans-migration factors also play a part in increasing or decreasing risk factors depending on the refugee child's length of time spent in transition camps. The impact of displacement on children has been observed in refugee camps worldwide (McCloskey and Southwick 1996). When a child experiences a lack of stability and safety, including constant disruptions to familiar routines over months or years in transition camps, this poses as a risk factor for increased risk of psychiatric morbidity, dysfunctional behaviour patterns or incompetence in work, love or play (Ahearn and Athey 1991). Refugee children frequently are severely emotionally and physically deprived, sometimes for long periods, prior to or during migration, or while in refugee camps (ibid.).

The experience of displacement (which commonly begin during pre-migration and continue through trans-migration into post-migration) contributes to multiple loss experiences. In the case of refugees there are the initial losses of a country, of a way of life, of family and friends, of social status, of profession or occupation, of emotional security, of cultural and religious acceptance and belonging, and of being able to interact and communicate with the wider society. Thus, when we relate these losses to Fullilove's 'psychology of place', as discussed at the beginning of this chapter, all three psychological processes (of place attachment, familiarity and identity) undergo monumental change. The effects of these losses are further compounded by the process of resettlement, and continuous stressors involved in adjusting to life in the new country.

Influence of post-migration factors on children

Adapting to a new country and culture has generally been acknowledged as a stressful process involving several interacting cultural, social, economic, language and environmental factors. For refugees, this process is compounded by experiences of trauma and loss, alongside multiple sources of stress such as financial problems, language, culture shock, racism, unemployment, health problems, changes in family structure and roles and different or little educational experience. All this can create individual and family disequilibrium.

Family themes

The significance of the young person's microsystem, and in particular the significance of the family, is often overlooked in post-migration literature. Nevertheless this dimension of the child's microsystem is essential to our understanding of the refugee experience. This is because for the majority of ethnic populations and cultures, the family is where themes of loyalty,

protection, obligations, responsibilities and plans are approached collec-
tively, and where the young person's psychological growth is influenced by
the family's unique characteristics. Yet through war and exile the family is
torn often unexpectedly and violently apart, leading to multiple losses and
uncertain reunifications.

From this family perspective, two main themes emerge. The first includes
family, culture and cultural transition, and recognizes that culture and ethnicity are intrinsic components of family attachment. Thus, exile can
dislocate the family's image and sense of unity. The second concerns family
trauma and family loss, and recognizes that some family members may be
killed or separated during war, and hence intact families rarely migrate
together (Chambon 1989).

The experience of exile, loss and transition disrupts the life cycle patterns
of interaction, roles, boundaries and inner codes of family members.
Migration in itself is so disruptive that it adds an entire stage to the life cycle
for those families who must negotiate it (McGoldrick *et al. 1986*). However,
among refugee families the separations are more sudden, more unpredictable
and more violent and the outcomes more uncertain (Chambon 1989).

A significant dimension of family trauma and grief, then, relates not only
to death or separation of family members, but also to the fragmentation of
critical dimensions of the family microsystem and the family life cycle. This
can propel the entire family system, or what is left of it, into disequilibrium.
Shapiro (cited in Silverman 2000) describes grief and loss as a family developmental crisis, interwoven with the family's history and its current
developmental moment. The family members' grief radically redirects the
interpersonal relations, family roles and future course of their life together.
In the context of the mesosystem and the broader social contexts of the
macrosystem in which the family lives, each family constructs for itself a
coherent system that guides, explains and accompanies its members as they
deal with the vicissitudes of life within these interacting systems (ibid.).

Some families have no language for loss or coping with loss within their
family's patterns of communication and meaning making, which makes
them more susceptible to subsequent stressors. When a family is flexible in
dealing with the effects of multiple loss and change within the family structure, for example, by acknowledging differences in grieving processes
within the family and accepting help, they are then more able to accommodate the new changes into the family life cycle.

Studies of refugee children have also identified a correlation between a
child's family support and the decrease or increase of PTSD symptoms. In a
study of Cambodian high school students in America who had survived
atrocities in Cambodia, 50 per cent were diagnosed with PTSD and 53 per
cent were diagnosed with depressive disorders several years after the Pol Pot
genocide years (Kinzie *et al.* 1986). Students who lost the family support
and culture of their pre-migration microsystem and who had to move into a

new foster care microsystem in their post-migration phase developed a higher percentage of psychiatric disorders. Those students who had experienced fewer disruptions to their pre-migration microsystem during the trans- and post-migration phases had fewer symptoms of severe trauma (Ahearn and Athey 1991). More general research conducted on children who have survived traumatic experiences estimates that between 45 and 60 per cent of these children will develop post-traumatic stress disorders (Cole 1996; Perry 1994).

Styles of coping with traumatic experiences

Themes of silencing, denial or minimizing traumatic events are often used by refugee survivors as coping strategies to protect family members from being overwhelmed (Almqvist and Brandell-Forsberg 1995, Montgomery 1998). They are particularly used in the parent–child dynamic. Children can be unwilling to share feelings or experiences of traumatic events in front of their parents. This may be for fear of upsetting their parents or because they do not want to acknowledge that their parents or caregivers, who may be their only wellspring of security, were unable to protect them from the traumatic experiences.

A parent on the other hand will often desire to re-create a sense of security and re-establish the child's belief in self and environment as quickly as possible after experiences of war, loss and trauma. There is consequently a desire to move forward and an unwillingness and fear around remembering, verbalizing and reactivating traumatic memories.

A feeling of security and belief in the parents' or main caregiver's ability to protect the child from danger is a critical foundation for the child's development of basic confidence in self and surroundings (Bowlby 1973). This foundation is also essential for healthy expectations and responses later in life and for developing and incorporating emotional, behavioural and cognitive proficiency. For these reasons, in war or other situations of extreme danger, family survival strategies such as minimizing, choosing to forget and denial are often implemented in an attempt to maintain the child's core sense of self, and the family as a constant, protective haven. Protecting a child from feelings of fear is commonly viewed by parents to be as critical as their role of protecting the child from actual harm (Almqvist and Broberg 1997).

Other aspects may contribute to the family strategy of minimizing or choosing to forget experiences of trauma. A number of parents and young people who have survived traumatic experiences of war, loss, persecution and exile struggle with feelings of guilt or shame. For example, they experience guilt at not being able to accomplish the parental mission or for being unable to provide help for others, which adds to the guilt of having survived. Feelings of shame are probably even more disturbing and difficult to talk about (Almqvist and Broberg 1997, Van der Veer 1998). Unprocessed guilt is known to be associated with post-trauma anxiety, while unacknowledged shame can show itself as feelings of unworthiness, anxiety about self-disclosure and embarrassment (Kaplan 2000).

Clinical practitioners frequently come across instances where the strategy of silence (that is, not speaking or not recalling) is used as a means of protecting the individual and the individual's family from shameful or powerless traumatic events. The husband tries to protect his wife, the wife her husband, the parents their children and the children their parents (Almqvist and Broberg 1997). However, this survival strategy gradually creates an emotional vacuum within the family structure and consequently mutual understanding deteriorates, because the different trauma experiences of each family member are not shared and validated. The family continues to function on an outward level, but the effects of trauma and consequent silencing strategies diminish the communication bonds, fragmenting the inner family resources such as emotional spontaneity and trust.

A study of Khmer refugee children found that parents also frequently underestimated the symptom level of their children and their social difficulties as compared to the children's assessment of themselves and their teacher's assessment (Sack *et al.*, cited in Montgomery 1998). These findings were thought to correspond with particular attributes of the East Asian culture; however similar findings were found among Croatian parents (Montgomery 1998).

In summary, minimizing, denial or silencing from war-related traumas are common coping strategies in refugee families (Almqvist and Broberg 1997). However, a balance is needed between maintaining a secure parent–child relationship where possible and creating the space for a child to be able to talk openly about war-related traumatic experiences. This is critical to avoid an acute crisis if traumatic experiences break through the protective shields within the microsystem (ibid.). If a family can be persuaded to restore contact with the past by talking about traumatic events, they will understand better how their experiences influence their present behaviour and be able to create new opportunities for supporting one another (Van der Veer 1998).

Loss, change and cultural bereavement

Culture plays a significant role in shaping and determining how an individual, family or community perceives, understands and copes with loss and change in life. It has been stated that culture becomes the glue that provides a community with meaning, cohesion and integration (Ahearn and Athey 1991). Culture influences not only how trauma and loss memories are remembered, but also how they are dealt with. In a local community in Peru, for instance, the people have a shared memory that is connected to the history of the community, while people in a similar community in Colombia have a very individualistic memory of traumatic events. It was found that the Peruvians have dealt considerably better with the effects of their experiences than the Colombians (Montgomery 2000).

Cultures carry with them history, beliefs, ways of doing things and processes of communication. Experiences of the most intimate events and the most public are interpreted by people, to some considerable extent, through their culture (Waldegrave 1993). Psychiatric data has shown that culture has minimal influence on early neuromotor and psychosocial development. However, later in childhood and in adolescence, many facets of development are influenced by culture. These include attaining literacy, courting, assuming adult responsibilities and achieving independent decision-making (Westermeyer, cited in Ahearn and Athey 1991).

As described earlier, when a person is uprooted from their primary social, environmental, spiritual and economic structures, this can produce intense and profound grief. However, it is an experience that does not necessarily fit into classic grief and trauma theories, but instead requires a specific form of cultural construction and therapeutic help, within the framework of the person's subjective experience of monumental loss. As a way of defining such loss, Eisenbruch (1991) has coined the term, 'cultural bereavement', which is the experience of the uprooted person or group, resulting from loss of social structures, cultural values and self-identity.

It is important to note that there are healthy and constructive components to cultural bereavement. Even if the symptoms resemble those of traumatic stress or other related illnesses, it is necessary to understand the meaning behind the symptoms and each survivor's response to personal losses from their cultural perspective. The significance of this is echoed by Waldegrave (1993) when he asserts that therapy is concerned with the manner in which people give meaning to experience and, in so doing, define their realities. But it is cultures which carry their people's history and meanings, and it is through these cultural meanings that events are interpreted for people.

If trauma and loss symptoms are therefore recorded without taking into account a more complete understanding of relevant cultural, mental and spiritual phenomena, then the assessment is divorced from the reality of the individual's or family's experience and its validity can be questionable.

Children and loss

It is important to note, when working within an ecological framework, that children's responses to loss cannot be understood independently of the interacting micro-, meso- and exosystems in which they live. There is, however, very little research or other related literature on refugee children's responses to loss, particularly when considering the diversity of contextual factors. The focus of the general literature and research on children and loss is primarily on a child's experience of loss through the death of an important attachment figure in the child's life. This research and literature nevertheless highlights some of the common developmental and social themes experienced by children who have survived a significant loss (Corr and Corr 1996; Silverman 2000) and is therefore relevant to the situation of refugee children. For instance, a child or young person's experience of loss is often not recognized or legitimized (Silverman 2000). This is further compounded by society's lack of awareness and patience around the process of loss and grief, leaving many mourners feeling demoralized and unsupported.

Children often experience deep and unfamiliar feelings, alongside a changed sense of being in the world and belonging to the world, after a significant loss. Younger children particularly may not have the experience to know that life will continue. Research in this area has found that a child's identity is more deeply affected by losses in childhood because self-development is still in progress, and a child's grief reactions appear to be longer in duration than those of adults (Corr and Corr 1996).

Despite this factor, a child's deeper responses to loss may not always be noticeable, and children will often express their grief, anger and fear in non-verbal ways. There may be the more easily recognizable reactions and feelings expressed such as temper tantrums, clinging behaviour, sadness, agitated searching behaviour or withdrawal. However, invisible responses can include a child's feeling of being lost or made smaller by death. Staudacher has observed that many child survivors of significant loss have described themselves as getting smaller and smaller – that they were so insignificant, so unimportant they might disappear (Staudacher 1987).

Developmental changes in children's understanding of death and loss have been studied by a number of researchers (Speece and Brent cited in Corr and Corr 1996; Silverman 2000). A common theme is the importance of understanding other developmental factors alongside a child's cognitive development. These factors can include the child's stage of separation; the level of maturity in the development of a sense of self, which includes the child's ego functions and ego defences; the child's ideas about the world; and the nature of the child's experiences in the world.

Neimeyer's (1998) constructivist view of grief and loss frames these themes. Neimeyer suggests developmental factors influence a child's way of making meaning from loss. Neimeyer describes human beings as meaning makers, striving to organize and anticipate their engagement with the world by arranging it in themes that express their particular cultures, families and personalities. This construction of meaning correlates with where an individual is developmentally, from both cognitive and emotional perspectives.

In general it has been found that gender is not a significant variable in a child's experience of loss or death. Age is the most common variable studied in children who have experienced the death of a significant attachment figure. Most studies have found that by the time a child is around seven years old they have a reasonably clear understanding of the concept of death (Corr and Corr 1996).

For children who have experienced multiple losses through war and exile, however, the experience is more complex because of the interaction of loss and trauma. It is believed that traumatic aspects of loss may hinder or complicate aspects of grief resolution because specific symptoms of trauma, such as avoidance, can interfere with normal processes of bereavement. Additionally, responses to traumatic and multiple loss are further complicated by the fact that catastrophic events affect entire communities (ibid.).

The child may not necessarily have experienced some of the more physically destructive aspects of war, such as witnessing persecution, death or destroyed houses and streets. Nevertheless, the sudden multiple losses of familiar surroundings, people, animals and objects, with which the child had a significant bond, can lead to the child developing intense anxiety and other traumatic symptoms.

Studies of children who have experienced bereavement and trauma have found it difficult to separate the symptoms of trauma from those of loss, because of the overlap between the two. However it is recognized that symptoms may be intensified because of the overlap. One of children's most common reactions to a significant loss is fear – fear of going to sleep, of being separated, of being unprotected and, for older children and young teenagers, of sharing feelings. Other common reactions are guilt, sadness, anger, withdrawal and confusion (Kaplan 2000; Staudacher 1987). Somatic responses, as discussed earlier, are common amongst pre-school children who have been traumatized, as is regression to an earlier phase of development.

A child's way of coping with loss

To understand a child's way of coping with loss, it is necessary to ask what of significance has been lost for the child. It may be a meaningful relationship with an important person or animal in the child's life, or it may be the wider ecological losses of home, street, school environment, special toys and familiar routines.

Children's grief reactions and coping responses differ from adults' responses. Nevertheless, Stroebe and Schutt have identified two common coping behaviours in adults and children. The first is loss-oriented behaviour, where the individual faces the loss and consequent grief. The second is restoration-oriented behaviour, where the individual deals with the new reality, and the need to change and find new roles and identities. (Stroebe and Schutt, cited in Silverman 2000).

In general most children are similar to adults in possessing a quality of resilience that enables them to cope and find meaning from losses experienced. Children's grief and coping are nevertheless more intertwined with their own ecological contexts and developmental processes, while also influenced more directly by how their immediate microsystem copes with loss. Silverman (2000) states that because the process is both reactive and interactive, the way a child moves or reacts always depends on the interface between the child and other mourners.

It has been identified that even a child of a very young age will attempt to make meaning out of the loss or losses they have experienced in ways which reflect their experience in life, their culture, their family and where they are developmentally (ibid.). In studies of young bereaved children, researchers have identified that young children are more likely to distract themselves, cling to familiar activities for comfort and use fantasy to cope, as well as to deny the loss for periods (Corr and Corr 1996). Older children and adolescents, on the other hand, have two main methods of coping which are in accordance with their developmental age: firstly, by using problem-solving strategies, such as reframing the problem; and secondly, by being able to regulate emotions, especially distress (Silverman 2000).

Whatever the developmental age of the child it is important to recognize that coping with loss and change is not something that is static. It continually changes in meaning over time as the individual matures, interacts with others, develops a changing identity and creates a new sense of meaning around the loss, while also utilizing new resources that become available.

Tasks of adaptation

Migration, discussed in more detail in Chapter 5, has been described as a developmental process with identifiable stages and developmental tasks, and which is influenced by life cycle, education and socio-economic factors. This developmental process of cultural transition is in addition to the normative developmental stages of the life cycle (Chambon 1989). There are thus dual developmental tasks in adaptation for migrants. For refugees, the tasks of adaptation are more multi-layered, due to the pre-migration circumstances of loss, trauma and major disruptions. Correspondingly, adaptation involves not only the individual and family, but also the wider social structures of schools and other institutions. Adapting to a new environment is therefore an interactive process involving multiple overlapping systems.

Life cycle factors mean the task of adaptation for older family members is sometimes to find their place in the ethnic community rather than become integrated into the mainstream culture (ibid.). This can, however, conflict with the acculturation needs of younger family members. Some of the more challenging adaptation tasks for spouses in the family system are to redefine the roles and perceptions of competence and authority. Role changes and differential rates of acculturation can occur when, for example, the wife finds employment outside the family while the husband, whose traditional role was the wage earner, remains unemployed. Issues around parental authority may additionally be an adaptation task when traditional ways of parenting do not correspond with the new culture and when parents attempt to control their children, for fear of losing them to the influences of the new society.

A refugee child's ability to adapt is influenced by the number of risk factors experienced, both chronic and acute, which can greatly decrease a child's ability to adapt successfully (Ahearn and Athey 1991). The ability to adapt is also influenced positively by protective factors that assist a child in coping; namely, the personality of the child, the existence of a supportive milieu and an external support system that encourages a child's coping efforts and creates opportunities for the child to experience success (Ahearn and Athey 1991; Van der Veer 2000).

One of the main tasks for refugee children within the school environment is to adapt and develop socialization skills in a new cultural and social context. Refugee flight almost always disrupts this process in two ways: first it breaks the continuity of the socialization process, and secondly it prevents the child from progressing normally in learning information and skills (Ahearn and Athey 1991). Within this context, one of the tasks for a refugee child is to incorporate and superimpose what is meaningful and functional from one culture to another (Eisenbruch 1991).

Schools have a part to play in this process by helping refugee children to feel less invisible through creating a safe, validating environment where they feel supported and understood. This includes recognizing and understanding that trauma can impede short-term memory and can interfere with the attendance process of learning. The school's task may also be to orchestrate learning experiences within the school curriculum that include refugee children's experiences and which reinforce positive ways of handling problems. The school can additionally support extra-curricular group activities for refugee students from the same or similar cultural background.

The impact of refugee grief and trauma on educational settings

There is currently scant literature on refugee grief and trauma in the context of educational settings, despite schools playing a critical role in the adjustment and mental health of refugee children. More general literature on children's experience of coping with extreme stress or traumatic loss within the school environment has documented that children have the competence and resilience to cope (Garmazy et al., cited in Silverman 2000). Other research has documented that school-aged children often seem to adults to change radically following a traumatic event. The child becomes irritable, rude, argumentative or complains of somatic problems, while school performance declines substantially (Ahearn and Athey 1991).

With respect to the experience of refugee children, it has been noted that generally they adjust satisfactorily to the new settings in which they are placed (ibid.). Nevertheless, research on refugee children and adolescents (Kinzie *et al.* 1986; Rousseau *et al.* 1998) has also revealed that a significant number of refugee children who have experienced loss and trauma exhibit emotional problems on resettlement. These differences reflect that refugees are not a uniform group and that each individual will respond to resettlement differently, depending on variables which include supportive social and cultural related networks, developmental differences, socio-economic status and the degree of trauma and loss experienced. Van der Veer (2000) notes that even a few good volunteers offering extra care, protection and coaching can serve as a protective factor which mitigates the stresses and trauma that young people can experience.

Such supportive measures are essential for fostering resilience and integrating the trauma and loss in a constructive way in a refugee young person's life. Rousseau *et al.* confirm in their data on Central American children that five years after resettlement in the host country, the children exhibited emotional problems associated with initial pre-migration trauma. The study of Cambodian high school students living in the United States, referred to earlier, found that half of the participants met the diagnostic criteria for PTSD and almost half met the criteria for other clinical problems, notably depression and anxiety disorder (Kinzie *et al.* 1986). Williams and Westmeyer also found that 60 per cent of the refugee adolescents they surveyed exhibited emotional problems (Williams and Westmeyer, cited in Bemak and Greenberg 1994). A recent analysis of Kosovar children arriving in Denmark showed that 68.5 per cent of the children had scores indicating a high risk of developing PTSD (Stoehr 2001).

In the school context, these factors all pose challenges to teachers, who often assume enormous importance to refugee children in helping them to deal with other, out-of-school needs. It has been noted that some teachers internalize the pain and trauma of their refugee pupils and become traumatized themselves, losing confidence in their teaching skills and doubting their own abilities, while other teachers may protect themselves by become rigid or distancing themselves (Fox 1995). Under these circumstances the task of the teacher can be a complicated one. Additional challenges for the teacher include language difficulties, differences in learning styles and educational experiences, cultural differences and lack of resources amongst many refugee families. Resilience has been connected with school-children when the child has experiences of nurturing caregivers, physical security, stable personality and a welcoming school environment (Cole 1996). Yau's research, however, has identified significant difficulties experienced by refugee students, which makes developing resilience more challenging. These include cultural disorientation, frequent relocations, difficulties understanding teacher instruction and gaps in foundation skills (Yau, cited in Cole 1996). Chapter 4 will deal with the issue of resilience in more detail.

Schools play significant roles in children's socialization process. For a refugee child this process is often violently disrupted in the home country, and does not restart until the child or adolescent starts school again in the host country. It is a process which is frequently at odds with the child's home environment and previous experience of school, where there may have been differences in discipline, school culture and processes of learning. This places additional pressure on a child who has already experienced multiple changes, trauma and loss. A study of Somali students in secondary schools in New Zealand found that students had to compromise their own cultural norms to succeed. They struggled with the ways in which learning is expected to occur and were marginalized not only by experiences of racism but also because of their low socio-economic status as refugees (Humpage 1998). Further, when looking at the mesosystem interrelationships, it has been found that a significant 'cultural distance' often exists between the culture of the home and the culture of the school. This gap is too great, at times, for many students to bridge. These children are often left to struggle and mediate the dichotomy between the two. Research has found, however, that the effective school will recognize this difficulty and helps the child and family to understand how the two realities can be accommodated (Cushner 1998a).

Assessment and care of these children within the school system is therefore an integral part of their schooling and requires clear programme planning to meet their special needs. This includes a differentiated approach to intervention, which validates different cultural frames of reference. It also includes supporting staff in understanding refugee experiences of trauma and loss, and providing assistance for teachers to manage their own fears and frustration when working with refugee students. With extra initiatives and effective interventions that emphasize the critical learning, psychosocial and cultural needs of refugee students, it is possible for these students to experience success within the school system.

Finally, if a child has been affected by the traumas experienced to the point where it is interfering with learning and adaptation processes, one of the tasks of family, school and related professionals is to offer therapeutic and social support. Family sessions are essential, because providing support to mothers in particular is a critical first step to treating the child (McCloskey and Southwick 1996).

Implications for best practice

As discussed earlier, when an individual is uprooted traumatically from their social, environmental, spiritual and economic structures, it can produce intense and profound grief. However, the refugee experience does not necessarily fit into classic grief or trauma theories, but instead needs to incorporate a specific form of cultural construction and therapeutic help, within the framework of the individual's experience of monumental social loss.

If we return to view Bronfenbrenner's ecological approach for assessing and working with the changing and interdependent environmental conditions on individual development (Bronfenbrenner 1979), it is imperative that refugee trauma and loss are viewed within these differential contexts. The significance of environmental factors such as the family, community and other support systems in helping refugees to cope with enormous loss and stressors cannot be overestimated. Through the interweaving of these factors it is possible to facilitate effective change and growth in refugee survivors. The suggestions for best practice that follow focus on assessment, therapeutic interventions, family and community involvement, and school, classroom and teacher practice.

Assessment

Assessment within this context presents a variety of critical issues. Refugee children have often experienced significant hardships before and during their flight, while the trauma experienced often affects the sensitivity of the brain to changes in the young person's environment. In addition, their trauma, loss and grief process needs to be viewed within the wider cultural context, which may alter the way these trauma and loss responses are manifested within the classroom. Consequently, it is valuable for any assessment to include an awareness of culturally-specific symptoms, as well as validating the meaning behind particular symptoms, so that some symptoms are not misdiagnosed or go unrecognized. For instance, in some cultures, distress and loss can be experienced primarily in somatic forms such as headaches, stomach-aches, or eczema. Anxiety can also be misdiagnosed in young people and can often present somatic forms.

Learning difficulties related to trauma are complex to assess in refugee children in the first months of arrival and any trauma-related reactions or blocks to social or learning situations need to be acknowledged and accommodated within a safe and predictable environment. However, when learning difficulties extend over time and the child fails to advance on a similar level to his or her peers, extra therapeutic support may be integral to the child's learning and development, given that attention and concentration skills can be significantly diminished by trauma. Within any assessment of the refugee child, there needs to be documentation of pre-migration and trans-migration stresses and significant events, as well as post-migration factors and critical events, given that causes of cognitive, affective or behavioural concerns can lie both in the past and in the present. In addition it is important during the assessment process to discern the coping strategies the child may have used to survive traumatic experiences. These may be cognitive or behavioural and involve processes such as dissociation, minimizing traumatic experiences, containing emotions within manageable bounds, problem-focused strategies or making sense of the experience within the context of a religious or cultural framework. It needs to be recognized, however, that some initial coping strategies such as dissociation can be mal-adaptive and place the child at risk of developing PTSD or Complex PTSD. Recent research has shown that the level of dissociation immediately following a trauma event was the strongest prediction of PTSD six months later (Shalev *et al.* 1996; Harvey and Bryant 1999).

Therapeutic interventions

All attempts to facilitate the refugee child's healing process through therapeutic interventions need to match the social and cultural context and include culturally sensitive activities. It is therefore important to obtain cultural knowledge relative to particular conflicts, learning and emotional or behavioural problems. Therapy also needs to recognize any healthy and constructive components to cultural bereavement. This is essential to the healing process.

Narrative therapeutic interventions, which include externalizing the problem so the child and the child's problems are not one, can be helpful when working with traumatized children. Art, music, dance, poetry or storytelling in the framework of the child's cultural heritage are expressive therapeutic tools for traumatized children, and help to integrate the past, present and future in a way that restores a sense of identity, meaning continuity, and belonging.

School and individual therapeutic interventions need to be interlinked to reconstruct a sense of social belonging in a way that validates their cultural identities. Consequently, both schools and families need to adapt and create a safe arena for supporting the child's transition. Recovery from trauma can only take place in the context of relationships; it cannot occur in isolation (Herman 1992). Therefore, empowerment of the young person in these social contexts is vital.

Family structure and function in each refugee culture needs to be understood and appreciated. Systemic and family therapeutic interventions are helpful in redefining and recognizing roles, expectations, relationships and responsibility in the family to ensure the family continues to operate as a unit, within their cultural frame of reference. It is also helpful to discuss the family's history and value systems and to help bridge significant gaps between the family culture and school culture.

School, classroom and teacher practice

Teachers have the potential to provide ongoing support for refugee students in a way that increases protective factors and fosters resilience. Teachers therefore need to be sensitive and responsive to the ways in which refugee children may be affected by their experiences, as well as the ways in which their trauma, loss and grief may appear within the classroom. This also requires some general understanding of the cultural reality of young people and some knowledge around how these cultural views can be expressed. Sometimes it can be difficult to determine when a refugee young person requires extra professional support. It is important, therefore, for teachers to participate in appropriate training and in-service activities related to refugee education and the effects of trauma on children within the classroom. These activities can be organized by specialist service providers within the community.

Integrating refugee children within the classroom may require both extra resources and additional mechanisms for supporting teachers as they develop their knowledge and expertise within this arena. It could be valuable to create supportive small group or department settings for teachers to discuss sensitive issues or any anxieties they may have when working with refugee youth. As will be discussed in more detail in Chapter 6, it is critical that the principal play a leadership role in supporting teachers in developing and accessing ways to increase their knowledge and understanding in this area.

Restoration of a sense of safety is a top priority for refugee children. The school needs to create a safe environment within the school and the individual classrooms. One approach within classrooms is the use of small groups, so children can learn from each other in an intimate and supportive environment. In addition, the implementation or strengthening of cross-cultural curricular topics and projects within schools could help increase levels of understanding, acceptance and mutual respect. Integrating a focus on human rights and refugees will additionally both inform mainstream students of the needs and experiences of the refugee children and validate the importance of the refugee children's experiences. Within this context, the development of extra-curricular activities would be of value – for instance, the development of after-school programmes for refugee youth who wished to participate. These groups could be places for the young refugees to express themselves through the traditional dancing or stories of their culture, or the groups could be used to address issues related to their experiences and to help rebuild a sense of the future for the young person (see Chapter 6 for more on how schools can adapt in order to support refugee children).

Finally, it is essential to foster positive and culturally appropriate liaison between schools and families which includes programmes for parents participating in school enterprises or school forums and where cultural diversity and communication is encouraged and validated. Parental involvement is essential for the academic success of refugee children. Without parental involvement or a supportive guardian, these children are at risk of failing and becoming further isolated within the school and wider community culture.

Chapter 3

Second language concerns for refugee children

Shawn Loewen

Language plays an important role in the task that refugees, both adults and children, face in resettling in another land (Burnett 1998; Watts *et al.* 2001). The newcomer's task of adapting to life in a new country is often complicated by the need to acquire a new language. Obviously, language is not the only concern of refugees in their new environment; however, one measure of refugees' overall success in adapting to their new environment is the extent to which they are successful in learning the language of their host country (Schumann 1986).

In order to gain an understanding of the issues concerning refugee children and second language learning, it is necessary to draw on several bodies of literature. Refugee children share certain characteristics with other groups of second language learners. They share the refugee experience with adult refugees, they share migratory experiences with other immigrants, and they share the educational context with other second language, as well as first language, learners. Consequently, studies and theories focusing on broader populations, such as adult refugees, immigrants or other second language learners, can be drawn upon. However, it is also necessary to consider what may be unique about refugee children, in comparison with other groups, in their task of second language acquisition.

Furthermore, in keeping with this book's theoretical model, this chapter will examine refugee children and second learning in relation to pre-, trans- and post-migration factors, with particular emphasis on factors influencing the task of second learning and good practice in the classroom.

In addition, this chapter will incorporate the ecological levels of Bronfenbrenner's developmental model. Primarily, the chapter will examine issues relating to the microsystem because it is this system which has direct influence on children and their second language development. That is to say, second language learning can be seen as occurring primarily when an individual comes into direct contact with the target language, either at home, in school or in other contexts. However, the influences of the mesosystem, exosystem and macrosystem will also be noted where appropriate, particularly when they influence, directly and indirectly, refugee children's opportunities for second language learning.

Pre-migration

One of the primary differences between refugee children and other learners studying a second language is the migration experience (see Chapter 5 for a detailed discussion of migration issues). In this regard, refugees are similar to immigrants; however, the lack of choice surrounding refugees' departure from their homeland and their arrival in a new country distinguishes them from other immigrant groups (Burnett 1998). Unlike immigrants, refugees have been forced to flee their homelands and have experienced varying degrees of emotional and physical trauma. These pre-migration experiences can then affect refugees during the resettlement process. Refugees are more at risk for mental health and academic dysfunction, and they do not arrive in optimal psychological or emotional condition for language learning. Indeed, some survival defences may initially impede the learning of a second language (Freire 1990). In addition, the lack of preparation prior to departure can make adjustment more difficult. In this regard, refugees differ from immigrants since immigrants usually arrive after much preparation (Coelho 1994), which may include study of the second language.

While the traumatic and stressful nature of pre-migration life may indirectly affect refugees' second language learning, other factors, such as prior education, may have a more direct influence. Studies of Southeast Asian refugees in the United States (Westermeyer and Her 1996) and Australia (Boua 1990) have found previous first language education to correlate significantly with increased English language proficiency after resettlement. In addition, pre-migration study of the second language correlated significantly (and not surprisingly) with post-migration second language proficiency (Caplan *et al.* 1991; Westermeyer and Her 1996). The implication of these findings is that refugees with lower levels of education in general and of second language proficiency in particular are at greater risk for inadequate second language development after resettlement. These findings are not encouraging for refugee children because many of them have had disrupted education due to the war and violence that have overtaken them (McDonald 1998). For example, the Khmer in Australia (Boua 1990) and the Somalis in New Zealand (Humpage 1999) arrived with little formal education and no literacy skills in their first language. This lack of previous educational experience makes the learning of a second language all the more difficult for refugee children. While little can be done to improve refugee children's prior educational experiences, it is important to be aware of this issue as these children are learning a new language (Rutter 1998).

Another important pre-migration issue is that the social status and experiences of refugees in their homeland may contrast considerably with their initial inability to communicate in their new surroundings. Some refugees have had above average interest and investment in the socio-political life of their own country; however, in the host country they may find themselves in a pre-verbal and pre-literate position that underscores their vulnerable and dependent condition (Freire 1990). Studies in Britain found that, unlike most other minority groups, refugees were often academically over-qualified for their jobs, but they lacked the language skills necessary for higher level positions (Further Education Unit 1994). A study of Southeast Asian refugees (Bemak and Greenberg 1994) found that poor second language skills contributed to feelings of isolation and depression. Thus, the inability to communicate in their new surroundings can compound the emotional trauma already experienced by refugees, particularly for those accustomed to much greater levels of involvement in society.

Trans-migration

The trans-migration period begins when refugees leave their home country and ends with their arrival in their host country. There are several language-related issues arising during the trans-migration period. Obviously, one issue concerns the length of time refugee children spend in a transitional environment. Related to this issue is that of education. If children are in transition for a relatively short period, then this may have little impact on their educational experiences. However, if they are in transition for a longer period of time, then it is important that they have educational opportunities. These opportunities may be offered in the children's first languages. Ideally, the children would also begin studying the language of the country where they will end up. However, in many cases this may not be possible because their final destination is not known. Minimally, then, children's education in their first language should be looked after.

Post-migration

It is also important to identify the tasks facing refugee children as they resettle in their new homeland. These tasks include learning the language and adapting to the culture of the host society, each of which will be examined in turn.

The task of learning the language raises the question of what it means for refugee children to learn a second language. While there may be several different answers, it is generally accepted in the field of second language acquisition that there are two types of second language proficiency: basic interpersonal communication skills (BICS) and cognitive academic language proficiency (CALP) (Cummins 1981, 1994; Ellis 1994). BICS refers to the language skills that learners need to engage effectively in face-to-face interaction, and it involves the mastery of contextualized language, which occurs in relatively undemanding communicative situations. By contrast, CALP refers to the linguistic knowledge and literacy skills needed to engage effectively in academic study, and it involves the ability to communicate precise, explicit messages in tasks that are context-reduced and cognitively demanding (Cummins 1981, 1994; Ellis 1994). While BICS may develop as a result of exposure to language through communication, the development of CALP is much more difficult. Collier (1987) found that it may take between four and eight years for children with low English proficiency to reach the average grade-level proficiency of their English-speaking peers. Similarly, Cummins (1994) suggests that it may take at least five years for English as a second language (ESL) students to achieve levels of academic English proficiency comparable to their peers who speak English as their first language. Since this review is primarily concerned with the academic achievement of refugee children, it is important to see the acquisition of CALP, not just BICS, as one of their goals.

In addition to the acquisition of linguistic proficiency, refugee children have the task of adapting to the culture of the host society. While acculturation is considered generally in Chapter 5, it is also an issue in relation to second language learning. Current theories in second language acquisition predict that learners will acquire the target language to the degree that they acculturate to the target group. Schumann, in his acculturation model, argues that acculturation, which he defines as 'the social and psychological integration of the learner with the target language (TL) group' (1986: 379), is a major causal variable in second language acquisition. Acculturation does not necessarily imply that second language learners must adopt the target group's lifestyle and values; however, learners must be socially and psychologically open to the target language group. Schumann proposes that second language learners' relationships with target language speakers can be conceptualized as a continuum of social and psychological distance. The greater the distance between the two groups, the lower the likelihood of learners acquiring the target language. Thus, social and psychological contact with the target language group, not adoption of the lifestyle and values of the target language group, is the essential component in acculturation.

According to Schumann, factors that may affect successful acculturation, and thereby the rate and overall success of second language acquisition, include the degree to which the two groups share the same social circles, the cohesiveness of the target language group, the congruence of the two cultures, the attitudes of the two groups towards each other, and the intended length of residence of the immigrants in the target group environment. Another important factor is the comparative social status of the two groups; the best conditions for second language acquisition are when the target language and the second language groups are of roughly equal social status, neither being dominant or subordinate.

Schumann's acculturation model for second language learning is reflected in current and more general theories of acculturation. For example, Berry (2001) identifies four major acculturation strategies available to immigrants and refugees, of which three correspond to strategies proposed by Schumann. One strategy, identified by both Berry and Schumann, is *assimilation*, which occurs when immigrants give up their first language lifestyles and adopt the host society's norms. This strategy maximizes contact between the target language and second language groups and promotes second language learning. A second strategy, labelled *separation* by Berry and *preservation* by Schumann, involves immigrants maintaining their first language lifestyles and rejecting the target language group. This strategy maximizes social distance and creates minimal opportunity for second language learning. A third strategy is *integration* (Berry) or *adaptation* (Schumann), and this occurs when immigrant groups adapt to the lifestyle and values of the target language group but maintain their own lifestyles and values for intra-group purpose. This strategy results in varying degrees of contact between the two groups and, as a result, varying degrees of acquisition of the target language. The final strategy, which is not included in Schumann's model, is *marginalization*, which occurs when immigrants neither acquire the norms and values of the host country nor maintain their own culture.

A similar theory of acculturation is espoused by Gibson (1988). She views acculturation as an additive process in which new traits and values may be added to already existing ones. For Gibson, alternatives to acculturation include assimilation, when individuals are incorporated or absorbed into another culture and thereby lose identification with their former group, and accommodation, when individuals publicly conform to host society standards to avoid or reduce inter-group tensions. Accommodation may occur even when the second language group believes that its lifestyle and values are superior. Again, language is only one part of the entire process of acculturation.

The preceding discussion outlined the nature of the tasks that refugee children face upon arrival in their host country. The following section will consider some of the post-migration variables that may affect refugee children in their task of language learning and adaptation.

First language issues

It is important to realize that all second language learners possess various skills and abilities in their first language (and possibly other languages as well). Too often a deficit perspective is taken towards second language learners, with the primary focus on the fact that learners do not posses fluency in the second language. This perspective can go even further, where second language learning needs are seen as representing a lack of intelligence or academic potential (Gunderson 2000; McDonald 1998). However, it is important to recognize the first language linguistic and literacy skills of second language learners and to build on them as much as possible (Waite 1992). One way schools can demonstrate that refugee children's language and first language identity are valued is by the provision of books in the first language (Bolloten and Spafford 1998).

Age

When it comes to children and second language acquisition, age is an obvious factor. It is popularly believed that it is easier for children than adults to learn a second language (Kennedy and Dewar 1997). In second language acquisition theory this belief has been termed the critical period hypothesis, which states that 'there is a period during which learners can acquire a L2 [second language] easily and achieve native-speaker competence, but that after this period L2 acquisition becomes more difficult and is rarely entirely successful' (Ellis 1994: 699). The critical period hypothesis is not, however, uncontroversial. For example, there is no consensus as to when the critical period ends, and recent research has suggested that the duration and nature of exposure to the second language may be more important than the age at which second language study begins. Ioup *et al.* (1994) found that native proficiency was obtained by two bilingual learners of Arabic after a period of 25 to 30 years in a naturalistic learning environment.

While the critical period hypothesis is controversial, studies of immigrant children have found age to be a significant factor in second language achievement. For instance, Gibson (1988), in a study of Punjabi immigrants in California, found that age of entry into the American school system was a significant factor in second language assessment of high school seniors. High school seniors who had arrived before fourth grade were more likely to be rated as 'fluent English proficiency' by the school system, while seniors who had arrived after fourth grade were more likely to be rated 'limited English proficiency'. Similarly, Collier (1987), in her analysis of the length of time necessary for students with limited English proficiency to become proficient in English for academic purposes, found the optimal age of arrival into the second language academic environment to be between 8 and 11 years old. Dufresne (1992), in a study of Hmong refugees, concluded that those who did not enter the American school system before fourth or fifth grade had little chance of competing successfully with their academic peers. Similarly, Boua (1990) concluded that Khmer refugee students arriving in Australian schools at the elementary level had better chances of succeeding in school than those arriving at the secondary level.

However, research does not indicate that younger is necessarily better. Collier (1989) found that adults and adolescents initially acquire basic interpersonal communication skills (BICS) faster than children; however, after two to three years of second language exposure, children achieve higher BICS. In regards to cognitive academic language proficiency (CALP), children between the ages of 8 and 12 who had several years of schooling in their first language were the most efficient. Collier also found that overall academic achievement was not affected by age of initial exposure to the second language as long as cognitive development continued in the first language until age 12. However, second language development may be negatively affected by discontinued first language development. In addition, if schooling is conducted exclusively in the second language, students require at least five years to reach the 50th percentile on nationally standardized tests. Collier concludes that consistent, uninterrupted cognitive academic development in all subjects throughout students' schooling is more important than the number of hours of second language instruction for successful academic achievement in a second language.

Social identity

Social identity concerns group membership, perception by self and by others, and the accompanying markers of identity (for example, language, religion and dress). As such, social identity is an important variable in second language acquisition because it can affect the amount and nature of exposure to the second language. Recent second language acquisition theories have come to view identity as multiple and complex, changing depending on the context. Certain identities may come into the foreground or recede depending upon the situations in which learners find themselves (Peirce 1995). Thus, second language learners may identify themselves with the target language group to varying degrees, with stronger identification being associated with increased second language learning.

Several studies have found identity to be an important factor in the second language learning process of immigrants and refugees. Gibson (1988) found that the Sikh immigrants in California viewed acculturation as an additive process. Therefore, the academic success of their children was not viewed as replacing a Sikh identity with an American one; rather, they were adding to their already established identity. As a result, even though the Sikhs had an oppositional identity to their host society, academic success, a trait which was associated with the host society, did not threaten that identity. Similarly, Caplan et al. (1991) found that Indochinese refugees isolated themselves from their non-refugee neighbours and maintained their traditional Buddhist and Confucian values, in spite of the perception that one of the goals of the public schools was to Americanize their children. Their beliefs, however, correlated with academic achievement and were entirely compatible with basic American ideas about the work ethic, motivation to succeed, and optimism about the future. Another study of Indochinese refugees in the United States (Skinner and Hendricks 1979) demonstrated that they shifted from an identity of 'refugee' to one of 'Asian American' as the usefulness of the latter identity in accessing resources became clear to them. Thus, their identity was shaped by categories which had meaning in the larger society.

While the focus in the second language acquisition literature is on shifting or maintaining identities, much of the grief and loss literature (see Chapter 2) refers to the loss of identity that refugees experience in their new homeland. For refugees this issue of identity may be further complicated by the need for emotional stability. The changes in identity that may be needed for optimal second language learning may threaten the coping abilities of individuals, thereby actually impeding the language learning process. For immigrants or other voluntary second language learners, it might be easier to accept the changes in identity; however, since refugees have little control over their circumstances, including some of the changes in identity, this may make it more traumatic for them, and create difficulties in accepting these new identities. Further study regarding this aspect of trauma and loss in relationship to the role of identity in refugees' second language learning is needed.

One further factor that may be considered under the heading of identity is relationship of the refugees to the host country. Gibson (1988) found that Sikhs in California used the idea of returning to India to legitimize continued adherence to their traditional values and to reject American values and lifestyles, even though there was little evidence that they would actually return to India. Similarly, second language acquisition by refugees may be affected by their perception of their status within their new society. If they wish to return to their homeland, they may be less motivated to learn a second language. By contrast, if they see themselves as settling permanently in their new homeland, this will provide extra incentive for them in their language learning.

Gender

Gender is another factor that has been found to influence second language acquisition. In general, studies have found that females are better second language learners than males (Ellis 1994). However, several studies of immigrants and refugees have found male gender to correlate with increased second language proficiency. Gibson (1988) found that Sikh males had a higher academic success rate in American high schools, which she attributed to differences in course selection and general responses to schooling. Westermeyer and Her (1996) also found male gender to be associated with greater English language fluency and with increased pre-migration education among Hmong refugees in Minnesota. Thus, in considering refugee children, it is perhaps less helpful to look at gender as a variable in and of itself, but rather to consider the opportunities and roles that correspond with gender in the cultures of the refugees.

Miscellaneous factors

Other factors which various studies have found to influence second language acquisition by refugees include lack of proximity to other target language households in the United States, not having any educational involvement in the United States (except English as a second language, or ESL, training), and not receiving welfare (Westermeyer and Her 1996). ESL training was not associated with eventual English fluency as determined by either self-assessment or objective language tests (ibid.). Similarly, Caplan *et al.* (1991) found two important factors in the academic achievement of Vietnamese refugees in the United States: the level of English proficiency on arrival and the number of children in the family. The significant finding is that educational performance is positively related to family size: the larger the size of the sibship, the higher the aggregate grade point average. They did not find any effect for English language and employment programmes even though they were provided in the resettlement programme.

Good practice

Now that some of the factors influencing refugee children in their task of learning a second language and adapting to their host environment have been examined, it is important to consider what schools can do to help refugee children in this task. Although this section is headed 'Good Practice', it should be pointed out that good practice may vary depending on the circumstances. Furthermore, individual variation in language learning is a well-recognized phenomenon (Skehan 1989) as is variation in refugee children's background (Rutter 1998; Hyder 1998). Consequently, what might be good practice for one learner might not be best for another. Similarly, what may work well in one context with one group of refugees may not work well in different contexts with different groups of refugees. Keeping these caveats in mind, the following practices have been identified in the literature as being helpful for refugee children in learning a second language.

Inclusive classrooms

The issue of including second language learners in mainstream or content classrooms has lately attracted considerable professional debate (Leung 2001a), with the consensus being that second language children should be included in regular classes with native speakers in most circumstances (Kennedy and Dewar 1997; Leung 2002; Mohan *et al.* 2001; Waite 1992). The benefits of placement in regular classes include the opportunities and incentives provided for the children since they are learning English for a purpose – to learn the subject being taught – not just for its own sake. Furthermore, children are motivated to learn English to participate in activities with other children, both inside and outside the classroom (Rutter 1994). If second language children are separated from mainstream classes, they miss the opportunity to interact with English-speaking children and their primary, and perhaps sole, source of English input comes from their ESL teacher. In addition, separating second language children limits their access to the curriculum (Rutter 1994), and labelling second language students can have a detrimental impact (Lewis 1998).

Part of the controversy around mainstreaming is in its definition and implementation. Cummins (1988) points out that most second language submersion programmes involve virtually no concessions to the child's first language or culture and, as a result, have well-documented negative effects for many children. Franson (1996) cautions that although inclusion may be the ideal, it should be well-planned and not simply implemented *ad hoc* to satisfy the latest dictates of theory. In New Zealand, Barnard (1998) cites *English in the New Zealand Curriculum* as saying that 'the transition [to the new school] is best managed by planned immersion experiences in mainstream English classrooms'(p. 6). However, Barnard claims that many mainstreaming plans overwhelm the student and are unsuccessful because they are poorly planned. Students and staff involved in a second language programme in Great Britain agreed that it was important to integrate students into the regular class settings in a phased and flexible way (McDonald 1998).

One of the theoretical supports for inclusive education for refugee children comes from Schumann's acculturation theory. Social and psychological contact with the target language group is essential for acculturation to take place. By denying refugee children the opportunity to interact with other children in class, educators are denying them a point of contact with the target language group.

While mainstreaming is a generally accepted practice, there is also a call for additional or supplementary programmes to help second language learners. For example, in England there has recently been tentative support for pull-out classes provided they are not decontextualized, but related to students' mainstream work (Leung 2002). Another programme in Vancouver, Canada, has provided additional support for immigrant students through introductory reception classes or pull-out classes (Gunderson, 2002). Another way of helping students is by having an induction process which combines 'diagnostic assessment, language support and tutorial guidance' (McDonald 1998: 163).

Davison (2001), examining ESL provision in Victoria, Australia, argues that the curriculum focus should vary, depending on several factors such as the second language proficiency, age and previous educational experiences of the learners. As seen in Table 3.1, Davison proposes multiple programming choices for the provision of language and content, based primarily on learners' second language proficiency. For example, students with high second language needs would have a curriculum focused principally on language development and would be grouped with similar students. However, these students would also have content integrated into the curriculum, perhaps as content in the language classes or by means of classes conducted in the students' first language. As students' second language needs decrease, they would experience more content-focused curriculum in mainstream classes. Their first language would play more of a supporting role, although students might wish to take 'foreign language' courses in their first language to continue developing their first language proficiency. Davison also considers the varying roles of ESL and content teachers, depending on the second language proficiency of the students.

Pull-out ESL classes

While including refugee children in mainstream classes is considered good practice, there may be some occasions where withdrawing them is appropriate. Reasons for withdrawal might include helping total beginners with basic English literacy, focusing on specific problems or assignments, and allowing traumatized students to develop a trusting relationship with an adult.

As is the case with mainstreaming, the benefits of pull-out classes accrue when they are well planned. First, it is suggested that any withdrawal be discussed with students and teachers (Rutter 1994). It is then important to focus pull-out ESL classes to meet the specific needs of the students and to link the classes to content courses in order to maximize relevancy (van Hees 1997). ESL students need to feel that these classes are meeting their needs. One way to do this is by concentrating on the skills needed and issues arising in students' content classes. If pull-out classes are not made relevant to the students, they may feel that they are losing valuable time that could be spent more productively in their content courses (Lewis 1998). Other students complained that separate ESL provision can lead to isolation and lack of contact with native speakers (McDonald 1998).

In order for there to be a link between content and ESL courses, there must be collaboration between the content and ESL teachers. For collaboration to occur, there must be positive attitudes and respect towards the role of the ESL teacher, something that often does not happen because of the lack of institutional status for ESL teachers (Franson 1996). Ideally, the ESL teacher should be seen as a partner with content teachers, and the developing of second language skills in students should be seen as the responsibility of all teachers, not just ESL ones (Rutter 1994).

Students in Gunderson's (2000) study reported that ESL classes were viewed differently by students in different socio-economic neighbourhoods.

Table 3.1 Mainstreaming: programming choices (Davison 2001)

ESL need	High	Medium	Low
Curriculum focus	Language (integrated with content)	Language/content	Content (integrated with language)
Role of L1 and L2[1]			
L1 maintenance orientation (continuing systematic L1 development)	L1-medium content classes/ESL with L1 support	L1-medium content classes L1 as LOTE[2] ESL with L1 support	L1 and L2-medium content classes/L1 as LOTE
L1 to L2 transitional orientation	L1-medium content classes/ESL with L1 support	Some L1-medium content classes/ESL with L1 support	L1 perspective
L2 support orientation (L1 used as incidental support for L2 learning)	L2-medium classes with L1 support	L2-medium classes with L1 support	L1 perspective
Timetabling options	Intensive classes; Similar needs ESL classes with some mainstream classes (parallel and adjunct classes, electives, self-access, focused group-ings, 'sheltered instruction')	Mainstream multiethnic classes with some similar needs/ESL classes (electives, self-access, focused groupings)	Mainstream multiethnic classes with flexible groupings
Student groupings	Similar ESL proficiency age/grade level L1 background	Similar ESL proficiency age/grade level L1 background L1/L2 groupings	Age/grade level L1/L2 groupings
Teacher roles			
ESL teacher	Direct ESL teaching; Collaborative teaching/direct ESL teaching	Team teaching; Collaborative teaching/support teaching in content classes	Resource for content area
Content teacher	Resource for ESL area; Collaborative teaching/support teaching in ESL classes	Team teaching; Collaborative teaching/direct content teaching	Direct content teaching

Notes: [1] L1 = First language; L2 = Second language [2] LOTE = Language other than English

Source: Mohan, *English as a Second Language in the Mainstream* © (1997) Pearson Education Ltd. Reprinted by permission of Pearson Education Ltd.

Students in lower socio-economic schools were generally more enthusiastic about their ESL course, viewing them as friendly and more welcoming places than mainstream classes, although they did complain about the prevalence of the use of their first language in these classes. However, students from high socio-economic schools, who wished to continue on to university, were quite negative about their ESL courses, viewing them as interfering with their academic learning. Furthermore, students who attended ESL classes were viewed negatively, as second-class students. Students also suggested that ESL courses should include academic content, and they felt that the use of the first language would help in explaining difficult concepts.

One other type of additional support that was used with success in one London school was extracurricular groups which met after school. Having this type of support group enabled the organizers to focus on particular groups of refugee students as well as making contact with the local community (McDonald 1998: 164).

Peer tutoring

Immigrant and refugee students who were interviewed in Canada overwhelmingly recommended that new immigrants practise speaking English with native speakers, and yet they themselves often found these opportunities difficult to come by (Gunderson 2000). One practice that has been put forward to deal with this issue is the development of a peer tutoring or 'buddy' system in which newly arrived refugee children are paired with both first language and second language peers (Barnard 1998; van Hees 1997). Because it is unrealistic to expect teachers to have much extra time to help familiarize newly arrived refugee children with the school system, it can be useful to have peer tutors to help new students become familiar with the expectations of their new school. Pairing a new refugee student with an English-speaking peer can enable the refugee child to learn how the system works. It will also give the refugee an opportunity to create friendships and to practise using English. In addition to helping the refugee, the English-speaking peer may learn from the refugee child as well, thus fostering mutual understanding. Pairing a new refugee with a first language-speaking peer who has been in the system for some time (if such a person exists) can also help the new student become familiar with the system, as well as provide support in the student's first language.

One account of two teachers who conducted action research projects involving peer tutoring (Lewis 1997) identified several important factors, namely that the training of peer tutors was very important; a shorter length scheme of six to ten weeks was more successful; younger children preferred same sex tutors; it was important to have common interests between the tutor and tutee; and, finally, that personality factors affected interaction.

Results of the peer tutoring included an increase in the amount and quality of talking for some second language students. In addition, both teachers and other students in the classes noticed a development in attitudes, social skills, and language awareness in many of the second language students *and* their tutors.

Another study (Samway and Syvanen 1999) of cross-age reading tutoring in Oregon and California found it to be particularly useful for second language primary students, regardless of their ability to speak, read or write in English. They also found that the tutors benefited by having the opportunity to be viewed as an 'expert', something Samway and Syvanen argue is rare for second language learners in English-medium classrooms. The tutors also benefited from having the opportunity to develop interpersonal and teaching skills and having experiences with English print that were authentic and comprehensible.

Samway and Syvanen indicate that a successful buddy reading programme includes initial and ongoing preparation of both groups of children as well as time for students to reflect after each cross-age meeting. Teachers of both classes need to be enthusiastic, and there needs to be a good selection of books that are in English, bilingual, and in the relevant second languages.

Cultural and first language support

In addition to learning how the new system works, it is important for second language children to feel that their first language and culture are valued and respected. This may be done through, among other things, giving students the opportunity to maintain and develop their first languages, although bilingual support may be difficult in multilingual second languge classes (McDonald 1998). This can be done by understanding second language children's language and cultural values and by supporting cultural diversity through incorporating the culture, language and experiences of children into the curriculum (Taleni 1998), especially refugees' values in regards to education, religion and world view (Humpage 1998). However, Jones (1998) points out that lack of funding often means that first language support for refugee children is non-existent and thus argues that the local community may need to be involved in providing this support.

Rutter and Hyder (1998) suggest that it is particularly important for refugee children under age five to be encouraged to use their first language with other children, their teachers and at home. Caregiving facilities should have a positive view of bilingualism and encourage expression in both the first and second languages. This will allow children to develop proficiency in the second language at their own pace and without undue pressure.

Another caution is that refugees should not be viewed as a monolithic community. Not all of the refugees fit the 'refugee' stereotype, and this needs to be taken into account in the classroom. Indeed, educators should realize that varying degrees of education, social status, religiousness, and so on exist within the refugee community, as Humpage (1998) found in her study of Somali refugees in New Zealand.

Classroom language

If refugee children are to attend mainstream content classes, one way that teachers can help accommodate them is by examining the language of the classroom. Comprehensible input is necessary for second language development. Krashen (1982), in his input hypothesis, argues that it is necessary to have input that is just slightly beyond what learners' know. Cummins (1988) supports the necessity of comprehensible input and argues that it is much better given in content classes where the second language is actually used to convey meaning, rather than teaching the language (often interpreted as grammar) as a subject itself. Some second language acquisition researchers (Swain 1985, 1995) have argued that comprehensible input is necessary, but not sufficient for second language learning, and that what is also needed is 'pushed output' – opportunities for second language learners to produce talk that stretches their competence because of a need to express an idea using accurate and appropriate language. Within the mainstream classroom it is possible for second language learners to have opportunities for both comprehensible input and pushed output. Teachers may need to modify their talk to provide more contextualized language for the students and they can encourage students to express themselves in language that may stretch the students' capabilities. Kay (1990), citing Cummins and Swain (1986), points out that much teaching involves decontextualized language. Kay argues that one way to help second language students is for teachers to provide context-embedded language as much as possible. In addition, recent studies (Ellis *et al.* 1999) of communicative language lessons (that is, where the main aim of the lesson is the exchange of information) have shown that teachers and students can take time out to discuss briefly the form of the language (for example, the meaning of a vocabulary word, the appropriate verb tense, and so on) without disrupting the communicative flow. Such focus on form is theorized to improve both students' fluency and accuracy in the language. Although no studies of content classrooms have investigated this, it is hypothesized that mainstream teachers and students can also take brief time-outs to address linguistic items, thereby contributing to the linguistic development of the second language students. According to Cummins (1988), the ideal programme is one with a bilingual teacher, modified second language input and first language literacy promotion.

Whole school environment

While specific teachers can do specific things in their classrooms, it is also important to consider the context of the entire school (Leung and Franson 2001). In terms of Bronfenbrenner's model, the focus now shifts from the microsystem to the mesosystem. Helping refugee children with the task of learning a second language and acculturating to the new society should be seen as the responsibility of all teachers, not just ESL ones (Rutter 1994). Indeed, Kennedy and Dewar (1997) found that New Zealand school principals and teachers felt that general school policies were an important part of effective ESL programmes. A policy of inclusiveness, a commitment to welcoming second language students and families and philosophical and administrative support for ESL teachers were all recurring themes in their interviews (see Chapter 6 for further discussion of successful whole-school environments).

Assessment

In order to determine if school programmes are effective, some type of assessment, both initial and ongoing, is necessary. Kennedy and Dewar (1997) point out that assessment can be problematic because it is time-consuming, it can be hampered by communication difficulties, and there is often a lack of suitable assessment procedures. Nevertheless, it is necessary both for initial placement and ongoing checks for progress. Becker (2001) distinguishes two levels of assessments. The first (which she calls district-level) is given to all students within the system and is used 'to make entry decisions, placement decisions, to monitor progress and to make exit decisions' (2001: 101). The second (classroom-based) is given by individual teachers in their classrooms to guide instruction.

There are several types of assessment that can occur. First it is important to identify if students are potential second language learners. Becker (2001) suggests an initial 'dominant language questionnaire' to assess if students need ESL support. Questions should query which language students first acquired, which language they currently speak most often and which language or languages are used most frequently by family members and caregivers. Once potential second language learners have been identified, assessment of students' second language proficiency can occur. However, it is important to test listening and speaking proficiency as well as reading and writing proficiency (Freeman and Freeman 1999; Becker 2001), particularly in light of the distinctions between cognitively-undemanding, context-embedded language (BICS) and cognitively-demanding, context-reduced language (CALP). This distinction may mean that if the only assessment of students' second language ability is made on BICS-type language, they may be overrated in terms of CALP.

Once the initial assessment has occurred, this score can be used as a base-line for comparison with ongoing assessments. It is also important to establish passing scores, if students are to be put into ESL classes (Becker 2001).

Often second language students are assessed not in relation to their own development and achievements but rather in relation to a monolingual English-speaking norm (Leung and Franson 2001). For example in Britain the trend has been to assess second language students using nationally-stan-dardized instruments, with local schools opting to conduct their own, often locally developed, second language assessment (Leung 2001b). Leung and Franson (2001) argue that second language assessment should be contextu-alized. They suggest both teaching and evaluating second language learners in regular classes through the use of tasks. Task-based teaching involves the use of tasks, defined as 'work carried out by a pupil, either individually or with others, within the curriculum context for learning purposes' (2001: 188). These learning purposes include both content and second language learning. Once it has been determined what types of tasks have been used in the classroom, these same tasks can be used for assessment purposes. It is then possible to evaluate learners' abilities 'to use language appropriately and effectively to accomplish a task' (ibid.) and to compare their language use with the language that would be expected to occur in such a task. Such an evaluation can provide a positive, contextualized measure of second language learners' abilities.

Outcomes

When discussing good practice and issues that affect second language learn-ing, it is important to keep the eventual goal in mind, namely, what do refugees expect of their new life, and what does the host country expect of its refugees? This issue may impact less directly on refugees, but as part of Bronfenbrenner's macrosystem, the ideology and expectations of a society towards its immigrant and refugee populations will indirectly affect refugee children's development. This debate takes many different forms in different countries, but it has implications for what will be viewed as a successful refugee resettlement programme. Cortés (1994), discussing immigration in the United States, suggests that 'multiculturation' should be the goal. The components of multiculturation include (1994: 25):

- mainstream empowerment acculturation – the development of the capacities of all students to function more effectively as part of the mainstream
- inter-group understanding acculturation – the development of the capacities of all students to function with intercultural knowledge, understanding, and sensitivity in an increasingly racially, ethnically, cul-turally and linguistically diverse society

- group resources acculturation – the development of individual and societal resources by drawing on, rather than attempting to eradicate, student ethnic, cultural and linguistic resources
- civic commitment acculturation – the development of students' sense of concern for and commitment to others and willingness to act on the basis of that caring in order to work toward a more just, equitable society.

In the New Zealand context, Taleni (1998: 28) expresses his concern 'about the strong assimilationalist policies in our schools, where all immigrants are expected to learn English, to learn in English and to fit into New Zealand society'. Clearly, this approach can create resentment and tension within the immigrant population and may interfere with second language acquisition and development.

Conclusion

In the end, it should be noted that second language acquisition is just one aspect of refugee children's task of adaptation. Language will contribute to their cultural development and their academic performance; however, their overall success in adapting to life in their new homeland will be measured by much more than just language, as can be seen by the scope of topics discussed in this chapter. The chapter has attempted to identify some of the pre-, trans- and post-migration factors which may influence the development of both first language and second language skills in refugee children. Furthermore, it has identified influences in the micro-, meso-, exo- and macrosystems which influence second language development.

Chapter 4

Resilience

Angelika Anderson

The literature on resilience is relevant to the education of refugee children because research into resilience seeks to discover how some individuals 'overcome adversity to achieve good developmental outcomes' (Masten and Coatsworth 1998: 205). It therefore offers an alternative focus – a focus on solutions rather than the problems – on identifying factors that promote good outcomes following challenging circumstances. Resilience is an attribute needed by refugees, because they certainly experience challenging circumstances.

The resilience literature also identifies risk or vulnerability factors. These are factors, which, if present in a child's life, will increase the likelihood of adverse developmental outcomes. Some such factors are highly likely to be present in the lives of refugee children (Werner *et al.*1996). Knowledge about how to foster resilience, either by increasing the resilience factors in the lives of these children or by minimizing risk factors, may lead to the development of appropriate interventions as well as providing information to better judge the effectiveness of interventions.

The relevance of the concept of resilience to refugees is apparent from the various definitions of resilience in the literature. For example, Blechman (2000: 92) describes it as '...the survival of a stressor (or risk factor) and the avoidance of two or more adverse life outcomes to which the majority of normative survivors of this stressor succumb'. The following is a more comprehensive definition of resilience:

> Resilience refers to the process of, capacity for, or outcome of successful adaptation despite challenging or threatening circumstances. Psychological resilience is concerned with behavioral adaptation, usually defined in terms of internal states of well-being or effective functioning in the environment or both.
>
> (Masten *et al.*: 1991)

In this definition, resilience is conceptualized in three ways: as a process, a capacity and an outcome. It describes the process of adaptation in the presence of significant challenges (risk factors, stressors), where a positive outcome (resilience) is facilitated by certain personal and environmental factors. Research into resilience has identified factors that are associated with good outcomes despite adversity (Blechman 2000; Garmezy 1991; Masten and Coatsworth 1998; Werner *et al.* 1996). As such it provides us with information regarding potential interventions to promote resilient outcomes. However, a list of factors is not enough – it is also necessary to understand the process of resilience (Freitas and Downey 1998).

There has been very little research into resilience of refugee children (Witmer and Culver 2001). Therefore this chapter will apply findings from the general research on resilience to the refugee situation. What follows is a conceptual description of resilience followed by a list of personal and environmental risk and resilience factors, organized within the model used in this book. That is, pre- and post-migration factors are considered as they relate to resilience and the different aspects of Bronfenbrenner's ecological model (Bronfenbrenner 1979, 1992; Garmezy 1991).

The concept of resilience

Overview

The term resilience is often used as a descriptor for people. Using the term as a label in this way leads to a common misconception that resilience is something people either do or do not possess. In fact, resilience is something that develops, and it only emerges as a result of adversity. Even some of the intra-individual factors associated with resilience can be described as acquired 'tools for good adaptation...shaped by interactions between children and their environments' (Masten and Coatsworth 1998: 205). Other predictors of resilience are contextual or environmental; for example, some children happen to live in more supportive environments than others. The important point in relation to refugees is that some tools can be taught, environmental scaffolds can be put in place, and resilient outcomes can be promoted (Luthar and Zigler 1991; Masten and Coatsworth 1998). Deliberately promoting the development of resilience is a desirable goal for interventions with people who have experienced adversity, such as refugees. Bronfenbrenner's ecological approach to development and the model developed in the first chapter of this book provide a context in which to discuss resilience and outline potential school-based interventions emerging from this body of research.

Developmental perspective

An additional source of confusion around the phenomenon of resilience stems from the fact that it has been researched from a number of different perspectives. One of these is the developmental perspective. Here, at-risk children are identified by the presence of risk factors in their lives; factors, such as poverty, low birth weight, perinatal complications and so on, that are statistically associated with poor developmental outcomes. In this sense resilience is associated with overcoming the odds; that is, developing normally in spite of the presence of a large number of risk factors (Masten *et al.* 1991; Werner 1993; Werner *et al.* 1996). The consideration of these kinds of risk factors is relevant here as there are likely to be, among refugees, children who could be described as at-risk even without the additional risks associated with being a refugee. Poor developmental outcomes for these children might be attributable to their at-risk status, rather than to the fact that they are refugees. This perspective also draws attention to the potential long-term developmental consequences of adversity for refugee children. As the literature suggests, it is the cumulative effect of a number of stressors that is critical in terms of outcomes. The kinds of risk factors described in the developmental literature need to be considered, in addition to any factors specific to the refugee experience, in determining the level of need or the at-risk status of a person (Garmezy 1991; McKelvey *et al.* 1992). These regular risk factors, likely to be represented in a refugee population at the same rate as in any other population, include contextual, environmental and individual factors, such as repeated childhood illness, divorce of parents and foster home placement (Werner *et al.* 1996). In addition there are a number of risk factors that refugees are more likely to be exposed to than other populations as a result of their particular circumstances. These include pre-migration factors (for example, prolonged separation from caregiver, absent father, departure or death of older sibling or close friend) as well as trans-migration and post-migration factors (for example, change of residence, change of schools) (ibid.).

Stress and coping perspective

A second conceptualization of resilience is portrayed in the stress and coping literature. Here, resilience is defined as '...sustained competence despite severely challenging circumstances' (Masten *et al.* 1991: 430). The risk factors considered are acute or chronic major life stressors, and the focus of research is much more on short-term functioning. Here resilience is defined as effectively coping and being able to deal with stress. This approach concerns itself quite directly with some of the pre- and post-migration experiences specific to refugees (experiences of stressful events, loss, and altered life circumstances) and the refugee's immediate way of coping.

Recovery perspective

The third approach conceptualizes resilience as the capacity for recovery. By definition, acute trauma overwhelms coping resources. No one is expected to maintain a high level of functioning, or to cope immediately, following extreme threat or disaster. However, over time the extreme trauma responses are expected to abate (unless life circumstances are permanently altered), and resilience in this case is the capacity for recovery (Masten *et al.* 1991).

The process of resilience

Research into the phenomenon of resilience shares the challenges of all developmental research, and that is the inherent difficulty of studying a dynamic and recursive process. It is important to understand some of the issues involved in this developmental process in order to draw conclusions about results of such research and assess their relevance for potential interventions (ibid.). Above all, it is important to note that causality can never be inferred from results of correlational research. Issues around the nature–nurture debate are also relevant to this context. Mostly it is acknowledged that the focus of investigations should be on the interaction between an individual with the environment (Freitas and Downey 1998). This is consistent with Bronfenbrenner's model as well as our model outlined in Chapter 1.

Resilience can be described as a process of development which results from stressful events or significant challenges. The process is an interactive, recursive one, in which both environment and personality play a part. The product of this process is the development of resources, both within the individual, and within the context or environment, or, as Blechman puts it, 'The capacity for resilience evolves over the life-span within the total context of developmental influences' (Blechman 2000: 94). Take the example of children considered as difficult. Difficult children might not attract the attention of potential mentors. They might also be less likely to have the opportunity to develop good social skills, or a positive view of themselves (Radke-Yarrow and Brown 1993; Werner 1993). Thus a difficult temperament might be predictive of a lesser capacity for resilience by limiting the likelihood that both personal and contextual resilience factors will develop in a person's life. These factors are already outcomes of the developmental process as well as predictors of further outcomes. However, within the context of a school-based social skills training programme, the development of social skills could still be fostered, and school counsellors could make it their business to be a caring presence in the lives of such children and thus alter their individual predicted developmental trajectory.

Resilience factors are at times quite situation specific (Cicchetti and Rogosch 1997; Freitas and Downey 1998; Luthar *et al.* 1993). Lists of common resilience factors do not necessarily apply to all people in all situations. For example, Cicchetti and Rogosch (1997) found that children who had been abused did not trust the camp counsellor, and thus did not utilize the environmental resilience factor of 'caring adult'. Instead self-esteem, autonomy, mastery and self-determination predicted resilient outcomes for abused children. Interventions for abused children, therefore, need to focus on fostering these intra-individual resilience factors, rather than providing environmental scaffolds in the shape of caring adults. Similarly, stressful events can erode personal resources in a way that the capacity for resilience becomes diminished. For example, depression in response to stress often leads to a deterioration of family functioning as opposed to poor family functioning predicting depression (Del Medico *et al.* 1996; Kaslow *et al.* 1994). An understanding of the dynamics of resilience is thus required in order to develop effective interventions, and give insight into why interventions do not always work. It also illustrates the importance of considering the dynamic interactions between potential resilience factors and environmental and contextual factors, as indicated by both Bronfenbrenner's model and our own.

The capacity for resilience

Under normal circumstances, psychological development is a highly buffered process (Masten *et al.* 1991). That means the kinds of factors that prevent psychopathology are present in most people's lives to a sufficient degree to enable them to deal with common challenges. In this sense we all have a large capacity for resilience. It is in the face of extreme challenges, those that exceed most people's coping resources, that only the resilient (by definition) escape adverse outcomes. Do these people have resources in addition to the normal buffering processes that help them to survive such challenges unscathed, or are they able to maintain existing buffers which for others would be eroded as a result of the challenging circumstances?

Traditional approaches to resilience concerned themselves with lists of traits and factors associated with resilience. More recently the focus has been on attitudes and cognitive systems that promote or perpetuate resilience, such as optimism, humour and control beliefs (Freitas and Downey 1998; Masten *et al.* 1991). It is those kinds of factors that enable individuals to consistently maintain adequate levels of buffers despite extreme levels of risks and adversity, and therefore represent a greater capacity for resilience. Blechman (2000) describes it as ego-resilience, which is a tendency to exhibit resourceful, flexible responses to novel or stressful situations, and is associated with children who grow through and beyond difficulties. High ego-resilience tends to co-occur with high levels of empathy, reasoning and problem-solving ability, conscientiousness and openness to experience. A question currently being researched is the relationship between having high levels of these attributes and the ability to create consistently more resilient circumstances. This approach would suggest that refugees who possess high levels of these traits should be better able to cope with the challenges associated with pre-, trans- and post-migration experiences.

This does not mean that people less well endowed with these attitudes and cognitive systems cannot achieve resilient outcomes to the challenges they face. However, they might need more external help and support in ensuring that their inherent resources are not overwhelmed by the demands of extremely challenging circumstances. Refugees are likely to have faced (or to face) extreme challenges. In addition, they are likely to experience circumstances that rob them of existing support structures and resilience factors, both internal and external. For example, a supportive family network might be lost through death, separation, displacement, or threatened by high levels of depression. A sense of self-efficacy, or internal locus of control, might be eroded by disempowering experiences such as victimization, abuse and the helplessness commonly associated with experiences in refugee camps (Ekblad 1993). Consequently, being able to identify conditions and factors which support resilience would be a central component of any type of intervention aimed at helping refugees.

The literature generally lists three types of resilience factors:

- individual, such as internal locus of control, problem-solving ability, agreeableness, self-reliance and good self-management skills, high IQ, physical attractiveness, a sense of humour
- familial, including healthy family functioning, a resilient family, structure and rules in household, family size (not too many siblings), required helpfulness (looking after younger siblings), shared values and a sense of coherence
- contextual and institutional, which includes supportive neighbourhoods, close peer friends, access to special services (including health and educational), additional caretakers, existing support for mothers outside the household, financial security, religious affiliations, positive school experiences, and the presence of a caring adult or mentor.

Resilience as outcome

What is considered to constitute resilient outcomes depends on the research perspective. In the developmental literature, resilient outcomes to developmental challenges would be normal healthy development, characterized by on-time attainment of developmental milestones in the cognitive, emotional, social and moral domains. The stress literature concerns itself more with immediate short-term outcomes, such as adaptive and maladaptive responses to stress, or 'effective adaptation in the environment' (Masten and Coatsworth 1998: 206). Maladaptive responses to stress are either externalizing responses (evidenced by behaviour problems, delinquency and the like) or internalizing responses (depression, suicidality and other self-injurious behaviours). Both maladaptive and adaptive responses to stress are seen as attempts by the individual to deal with the situation, and so are essentially functional (at least in the short term). Resilient outcomes in this case can be promoted by reducing the stress and/or training alternative, adaptive coping responses. Adaptive coping responses, according to Blechman (2000), are always essentially pro-social.

Lastly, in cases of acute or prolonged adversity where trauma is evident and any sense of maintained functioning is unlikely, resilient outcomes are associated with good recovery from trauma (see Chapter 2). Trauma symptoms in children are similar to those in adults and the best predictor of short-term trauma symptoms is the psychological proximity of the threat to the child. That is, children whose immediate family has been under direct threat are more likely to suffer symptoms than children whose more distant relatives have experienced threat. In addition children are also affected by the way their parents respond to the threat, or by the way that parenting patterns might be altered as a result of the parents' experiences of threat (Masten *et al.* 1991).

A call for caution

Resilient children – those who have overcome adversity more successfully than the norm – are not invulnerable. The resilience that has developed is not a permanent guarantee that the same individuals will not ever be overcome by some future adversity. Even resilient people have limits to their resources. When they encounter circumstances that overcome these resources, they, too, will be overwhelmed by them.

In addition, having survived adversity does not mean that these people do not bear any scars. Some suggest that resilience creates its own vulnerability. Even resilient children need help and support to overcome the sadness and the loss of trust resulting from their experiences (Garmezy 1991; Luthar *et al.* 1993).

Finally, the development of resilience can be quite domain specific. Just because a person responded with resilience to one specific situation does not mean that the same person will exhibit the same resilience in a different situation. Also, different situations might require different kinds of resources. Known resilience factors may not function as such for all people in all situations (Cicchetti and Rogosch 1997; Del Medico *et al.* 1996; Luthar *et al.* 1993).

Issues specific to refugees

There are not many studies that have researched resilience in the context of the refugee experience (Witmer and Culver 2001). However, many specific risk factors that refugees are likely to encounter are well-known. Pre-migration factors include experiences of war, famine, persecution, violence, flight, loss of home, loss of family and friends, loss of a way of life and involuntary migration. Current and ongoing factors of the refugee situation might also affect coping. Ekblad (1993), for example, suggests that the socio-cultural context of refugee stress may play a considerable role. The culture of origin may determine what is experienced or interpreted as stress, the appropriate ways of coping, and the kinds of coping strategies available. Therefore, one needs to be cautious about the generality of both known risk as well as resilience factors where refugees are concerned. It is important to consider how the specifics of the host environment interact with what refugees bring to the situation.

An additional source of stress for refugees might be a disjunction between such expectations in the culture of origin and the host culture. Some factors which might serve as resources in the home culture might represent a stressor in the host culture. For example, church affiliation is cited in the literature as a resilience factor. However, if a strong church affiliation serves to alienate the new immigrant from the host culture, this might turn into a risk factor. Similarly, a higher parental educational status is usually associated with better outcomes for children. For refugees, however, this is not the case, probably because highly educated refugees rarely find employment at their level in the host nation, and the resulting loss of status has negative side-effects (such as depression, loss of self-esteem) which impact adversely on the children in the family (Montgomery 1996).

Refugees are highly likely to experience a large number of known stressors or risk factors at a time when, as a result of their experiences and by displacement, they are also removed from many of their existing contextual and personal resources. The literature emphasizes that it is not any one individual stressor that is particularly damaging, but the cumulative effect of a number of stressors. Compared with the stressors associated with migration, for example, refugees encounter many more stressors before, during and after the flight, and are deprived of more protective factors (Hodes 2000). When refugees finally arrive in the host country, they find themselves in a situation where they are likely to have limited access to contextual support (friends, a supportive neighbourhood and so on) and where even well-developed personal resilience factors (such as good social skills) might be of limited use without language or cultural competencies in the host country. Therefore, the refugee situation is likely to challenge even those individuals who had developed resilience previously in their home country.

Specific risks and resilience factors for refugee children

A recent large-scale study of refugee children in the United Kingdom suggested that up to 40 per cent of those children were affected by some sort of psychiatric disorder (depression, post-traumatic stress disorder and other anxiety-related difficulties) as a result of their experiences (Hodes 2000). With so many children affected, host countries need to develop sound strategies to address their needs. For these children, whose parents may themselves be distressed and unaware of their children's distress, contextual supports in the host country may be the only environmental resilience factor left. For refugee children, schools may well be the first and only point of contact between the refugee child and the host community, and hence potential environmental or ecological support. School-based services for refugees can be targeted at treatment, as well as primary and secondary prevention (ibid.). Successful interventions often require a multidisciplinary approach and collaboration between mental health, social service departments, and education (ibid.).

For new immigrants, schools are one of the more consistent points of contact with the host culture. As such schools are in a powerful position to impact positively on the lives of refugees. Schools have been identified as a potential source of resilience provided people have positive experiences there or find there a mentor, teacher, or other caring adult (Werner 1993). In addition to this, schools can do a lot to promote resilient outcomes for refugees by facilitating the development of both personal and contextual resilience factors in their lives. Specific suggestions for how this can be accomplished are presented in the conclusions to this chapter.

Some sub-populations of refugee children might be particularly vulnerable. There is some evidence, for example, that disorders associated with the refugee experience, such as post-traumatic stress disorder (PTSD), cluster in families. Hodes found that adolescents with at least one parent with PTSD were more likely to also have PTSD than others with similar experiences (Hodes 2000). Hodes also suggested that there might be a genetic susceptibility for PTSD. This represents a double disadvantage for the children concerned, since the most needy children are also least likely to have parents able to help and support them. In addition, parental psychological difficulties generally are also associated with a variety of disturbances in children, such as emotional disturbance and adjustment difficulties, including academic underachievement (ibid.). This adds to the argument for the need of contextual support for refugee children.

Conversely, there is also some evidence that the children themselves might at times be the source of resilience factors for their parents and communities under certain circumstances (Hinton 2000). Children in Bhutanese refugee camps, for example, have been shown to be active participants in their communities, bringing ideas and messages into the households that were listened to and respected by the adults (ibid.). Therefore interventions aimed at children might represent resilience factors for vulnerable adults, families and communities in some cultures, particularly, perhaps, those for whom the western, clinical model of stress, developed in individualistic societies, is not appropriate. Child-centred and culturally sensitive approaches however, are rare to date (ibid.).

Conclusion

The resilience literature offers a dynamic and comprehensive perspective on the refugee situation, and has a positive focus on good outcomes and possible interventions. Though little can be done about what occurred in the past in the lives of refugees, knowledge of the refugee's pre-migration experiences and contexts will give a clearer picture of a particular child's at-risk status, and hence level of need. It might also offer insight into appropriate buffers or scaffolds that might be implemented or offered to help the child successfully adapt to a new set of circumstances. Interventions can be put in place to enhance or add to the factors that already exist in the environment to promote the development of resilience. School-based interventions could be structured such that known environment-based resilience promoting factors could be put in place, and all would benefit. Potential school-based interventions include:

- ensuring there is a caring adult or mentor available
- ensuring there is a nurturing, accepting and caring school climate characterized by tolerance and acceptance, and which includes structured opportunity for social interaction (peer support programmes and so on) in order to maximize the opportunity for newcomers to make friends and find a supportive social network
- developing programmes or philosophies that promote the development of personal resources such as self-esteem, internal locus of control, and good social skills
- teaching the host language to both children and adults to facilitate the development of social networks and decrease the likelihood of role-reversal, which could threaten family functioning
- developing social networks further by organizing school-wide activities, allowing refugees to meet local people, as well as each other
- ensuring counsellors and teachers are aware of the children's needs and make themselves available as a potential friend or mentor
- using group processes in class to facilitate the development of friendships for refugees
- making local information available to alleviate some of the stress associated with relocation.

This chapter has attempted to describe resilience as a process, a capacity and an outcome within our dynamic and ecological model of refugee adaptation. Refugee children are highly likely to be at risk for adverse developmental outcomes, including academic underachievement and externalizing and internalizing behaviour problems, as they attempt to cope with the multitude of stressors in their lives in a situation where they are likely to have the benefit of very few effective environmental or personal resources.

Schools can assist refugee children in a number of ways as outlined above. They can help the children deal with the effects of the traumatic experiences they have had in the past and recognize that some refugee children might have great needs for therapeutic interventions (see Chapter 2). Schools can also help reduce the stress the children are experiencing by smoothing the transition into the unfamiliar new school and by facilitating the development of social support networks. In order to be effective, schools need to recognize that some of the children's maladaptive responses are attempts to cope with a very stressful situation, and that they require education and therapy rather than punitive measures. Effective support will also require knowledge of and sensitivity to the specific culture of a given refugee population whose needs can differ from those of members of other cultural groups. Schools have the potential to be either another risk factor, or to become a resilience factor in the lives of refugee children.

Chapter 5

Issues of migration

Angelika Anderson

A central feature of the refugee experience is migration; that is, movement from a familiar place, 'home', to a different place, usually a foreign country and culture. The following chapter deals with issues shared by people who migrate, including refugees, and who therefore experience displacement and often contact with another culture as well. It will outline the factors that are associated with displacement and acculturation that impact on the process of adaptation to a new place. The chapter first examines two general theoretical frameworks relating to displacement and acculturation and then relates these to the specifics of the refugee situation in terms of the model outlined in Chapter 1 of this book. To this end pre-migration, trans-migration and post-migration factors will be considered and how they affect refugees' ability to successfully accomplish the tasks faced in adapting to a different place and a different culture. These issues will be considered within an ecological perspective that takes account of personal factors embedded in the physical and the social environment, as detailed in Bronfenbrenner's model of human development. Therefore, unlike Chapter 2, which focused on the effect of migration on individuals in terms of loss, grief and trauma, this chapter focuses more on the nature of interactions between individuals and their environments and the between- and within-group processes as they affect adaptation. Issues will be discussed in terms applicable to all migrant populations as well as in relation to the refugee situation specifically.

Displacement

The effects of displacement on people's psychological well-being have been studied from a number of theoretical perspectives, including the 'psychology of place' (Fullilove 1996) (see also Chapter 2) and stress theories (Ekblad 1993). Displacement involves a great deal of disruption to everyday life. Even moving house within the same town can be stressful. There is a loss of attachment, routines and the ease associated with familiarity, and a need to orient oneself in a new space, establish new routines, and develop a positive identity associated with the new locality. Refugees have to cope with the stresses associated with physical upheaval under the worst imaginable set of circumstances, without being able to prepare for it, often without hope of ever being able to return to their home place – all this at a time when their personal, social and material resources are already likely to be exhausted.

The saying 'home is where the heart is' reflects common notions of 'home' as a place of emotional security which is part of our identity and where we 'belong'. The 'psychology of place' considers the importance of a physical locality for psychological health. It assumes that all individuals strive for a sense of belonging to a place in terms of three psychological processes: familiarity, attachment and identity. A 'good enough' home (ibid.) functions as a geographical centre which allows us to be productive and creative, giving expression to our selves. 'Toxic environments' (Fullilove 1996: 1517), on the other hand, threaten health and survival. Loss of home may lead to 'nostalgia' and 'homesickness' (Ekblad 1993; Fullilove 1996; Vantilburg *et al.* 1996). Encouraging a sense of belonging following migration is seen as an important goal of recovery efforts (Fullilove 1996).

Stress theories focus on the stresses associated with relocation. The demands placed on the individual by the need to adjust to a new environment are, by definition, stressful. This is apparent from the following definition of 'stress' by Ekblad where '…"stress" denotes stereotyped physiological "strain" reactions in the organism when it is exposed to various environmental stimuli, changes in, or pressures and demands to adjust to, the environment' (Ekblad 1993: 160). The extent to which people are able to accomplish the task of successfully settling into a new place depends on a number of factors including pre-migration experiences, personal resources, social networks, contextual and cultural elements, and potential ongoing stressors. Refugees will carry the effects and memories of pre-migration and trans-migration experiences with them to the new place, where they affect the individuals' ability to adapt to the new situation. Refugees might also bring with them more or less intact social support networks including family. In the new place they encounter a host of factors that will either impede or aid the process of adaptation. The factors the refugees bring to the situation, the factors they encounter in the new situation and the task of adaptation itself, and what might be done to facilitate positive outcomes to the process of adaptation will be discussed in more detail.

Pre-migration factors: what refugees bring

Many of the pre-migration factors which impact on refugees' ability to deal with the task of successfully relocating have been discussed in Chapter 2. These are experiences of trauma, loss and grief that are a part of the total refugee experience, and the impact they have on individuals, their personal coping resources and hence their ability to adapt. Personal resources, such as flexibility, good health, decision-making strategies, adaptability, social skills, an internal locus of control and so on, have a direct impact on the refugee's ability to adjust to the new locality (Vantilburg *et al.* 1996). In addition, refugees might also bring with them social support structures and contextual factors that could help them relocate successfully. These can include intact family units or close friends and neighbours who all make the same journey.

Pre-migration factors which impact negatively on children's ability to adapt to a new place include the cultural distance between the home and the new place (ibid.). Factors specific to refugee populations include things such as experiences of direct violence, an apathetic or unstable mother (parental mental health), a higher educational level for the father, separation from a parent and a lack of information about the flight (Ekblad 1993). Factors that act as a buffer include an optimistic mother and having social support (Ekblad 1993; Montgomery 1996). Interestingly, though a high parental educational level is generally associated with better outcomes for children (for example, Werner 1993), for refugee children this appears not to be the case. This is because for these parents a high level of education is not necessarily associated with employment in well-paid, high status jobs in the host country (Ekblad 1993; Kanal and Adrienne 1997; Montgomery 1996).

Post-migration: the task

Part of the task the refugees face is that of settling into a new place, and orienting themselves in a new location. To begin with, the refugees need to come to terms with their situation, which includes coping with the loss of their home and familiar way of life (Vantilburg *et al.* 1996). The process of adapting to a new place and lifestyle includes finding one's bearings geographically, and getting used to different ways of doing things. Schoolchildren have to get used to a new route to school (maybe even new and unfamiliar modes of transport) and find their way around that new school geographically as well as negotiating their way through its organizational and social structures. Adapting to a new place also involves the process of establishing new social networks, making friends, forming new attachments and developing a healthy sense of belonging to the new place (Fullilove 1996). All these things can only be accomplished if the demands of the situation do not outweigh the coping resources of individual refugees.

Interfering and facilitating factors

Some potential barriers and facilitators to the task of adaptation may be inherent in the new geographical and social environments. Existing structures within a locality (including schools) might either hinder or facilitate the accomplishment of the adaptation task faced by refugees. Potential facilitating factors include the availability of introductory orientation programmes to the new country (and school), along with existing procedures to welcome newcomers, and attitudes in the local population such as acceptance of diversity, inclusiveness, warmth and friendliness. Conversely, local structures and attitudes might be such that they represent barriers (Ekblad 1993; Fullilove 1996; Vantilburg *et al.* 1996).

In addition, the geographical and cultural distance between the place of origin of the refugees and the host nation and the voluntariness of the migration are important predictors of outcomes. Forced migration (which applies to refugees) particularly is often associated with vulnerability, poverty, dependence and helplessness (Ekblad 1993; Vantilburg *et al.* 1996).

How to facilitate adaptation

Environmental barriers and facilitators are amenable to intervention. Facilitators can be developed and barriers can be removed. Fullilove (1996) suggests it is essential to help refugees to re-establish a health-promoting habitat and affirm their sense of belonging. To do this one needs to ensure that people live in a 'good enough' (ibid.: 1517) place, feel settled at home and in the neighbourhood, contribute to the caretaking of the environment (both personal and shared), know their neighbours and interact with them to solve communal problems. This can be achieved in a series of steps including working together to rebuild former activities, attending to shared emotional needs, such as mourning the lost place, and maintaining rituals of the old place as well as participating in the rituals of the new place (Fullilove 1996).

Schools are major socializing agents and points of contact between the refugees and their new country. Schools play a vital part in helping immigrant children understand the new country, find social support, gain access to trusted people and experience acceptance. This enables them to become a meaningful part of their new home (Vantilburg *et al.* 1996).

Outcomes and consequences of migration

Homesickness, depressive and somatic symptoms as a result of relocation are most frequent among children (Ekblad 1993). Developmental delays due to the disruption and difficulties in adapting to a new environment are also common among children (ibid). 'Nostalgia', by definition, is the sadness that comes from longing for a familiar place (Fullilove 1996). This kind of sadness will impede refugees' ability to adapt to a new place, as well as affecting their functioning in general (Vantilburg *et al.* 1996). These are the negative outcomes associated with migration in terms of a change of locality.

The successful integration of the immigrants into a new country requires that they are able to participate fully in its activities, be economically independent and be settled in terms of having a sense of belonging. For children this includes acquiring the host language so that they can fully and successfully participate in school life and become a meaningful part of the new place. For parents and children to be able to achieve this, every attempt must be made to maintain and/or establish normal and adpative patterns of functioning. This will clearly require intervening at multiple levels within the ecology of the family and child.

Acculturation

The previous section dealt with issues around one aspect of migration, namely displacement. Another aspect of migration is that it often leads to contact with a different culture. The following section examines the process of adaptation to a different culture from two slightly different theoretical perspectives. The two theories will be described in general terms and then as they relate to refugees. Implications will be discussed in terms of how pre-migration, trans-migration and post-migration affect the process of acculturation.

The term acculturation refers to the cultural changes that occur when two or more cultures come into contact. The psychology of acculturation 'seeks to understand continuities and changes in individual behaviour that are related to the experience of two cultures through the process of acculturation' (Berry 1995: 457) and is distinct from the main body of cross-cultural psychology, which concerns itself with comparative examinations of psychological similarities and differences between members of different cultural groups. This latter approach, which links individual behaviour to membership of a culture is also relevant to the treatment of refugees, particularly in relation to trauma, stress and culturally appropriate interventions. Some of the relevant issues have been highlighted in Chapter 2 of this book. This present section limits itself to a discussion of 'acculturation' as defined above and as distinct from 'displacement', because migration is not a necessary requirement for cross-cultural contact.

Theories of acculturation

When people from more than one cultural group meet, a number of within- and between-group processes come into play that affect the developmental course of individuals and groups and their behavioural adaptations during the process of acculturation. These adaptations are both the outcome as well as the predictor of development. Acculturation was first studied within anthropology where the focus was primarily on group-level processes (for example, Mickelson 1993). More recently a focus on the psychological aspects of acculturation has led to the development of theoretical frameworks that focus on the adaptation of individuals during the process of acculturation (Berry 1987, 1995, 1999, 2000, 2001).

Culture is a central aspect of people's life. Berry suggested that '...all human behavior is cultural in some respects; virtually no psychological phenomenon can be independent of the cultural context in which it developed, and is now displayed' (Berry 1999); or, in Ogbu's words, 'Culture is a people's way of life' (Ogbu 1995b: 192).

Psychological acculturation 'refers to the process by which individuals change, both by being influenced by contact with another culture and by being participants in the general acculturative changes under way in their own culture' (Berry 1995: 460). Berry has developed a model that considers issues of acculturation at the individual, the institutional and the national level in both the host culture and the acculturating group and how they affect the behavioural adaptations of both groups. Certain configurations of attitudes in the acculturating group and the host society predict more or less adaptive outcomes, which are associated with varying degrees of acculturative stress.

This section will briefly describe these models. This is followed by a discussion of the implications for refugees, specifically how pre-migration, trans-migration and post-migration experiences of refugees impact on the process and potential outcomes of acculturation. Outcomes and possible interventions will be discussed.

Models of acculturation

When refugees arrive in a new host country, they typically do so in groups. Even if they make the journey as individuals or in small family units, because their flight has usually been triggered by factors that affect their whole nation or region of origin, they are likely to find themselves as members of a group of migrants who have come to a new place for the same reason. As such refugees will typically constitute a more or less cohesive minority group whose members share significant characteristics within a host country. For this reason both theories – those that focus on the group processes as well as those that focus more on individual adaptations – need to be considered in describing the task of acculturation faced by groups of refugees when they arrive in a new country.

In most culture contact situations the groups involved are not of equal status. Generally speaking one group is dominant (the 'donor' culture) and the other one is the acculturating group (the receptor) which is expected to undergo the most changes as a result of the contact. In the case of refugees it is likely that the refugee group will be the one with minority status, and the host country will be the donor culture. Factors known to affect the course of acculturation in both cultures include the following: purpose of the contact (for example, migration for economic reasons, or invasion for the purpose of colonization); length of contact; permanence of contact; size of the populations; policies of the populations (pluralistic goals versus strategies for assimilation, for example); and cultural qualities (for example, how traditional or flexible the cultures are) (Berry 1987, 1995; Bishop and Glynn 1998; Cushner 1998a; Ogbu 1995a, 1995b). One factor considered to be an important predictor of outcomes from a number of perspectives is the voluntariness of the cross-cultural contact (Berry 1987, 1995; Ogbu 1995a, 1995b).

For refugees the situation is such that their migration is usually involuntary (Kaprielian-Churchill 1996). In addition refugees often do not have the option of returning home. These factors predispose refugees towards the development of an oppositional cultural frame of reference (Ogbu 1995a, 1995b) and negative acculturation attitudes (Berry 1987, 1995), both of which are predictive of negative outcomes. An oppositional cultural frame of reference refers to ideal ways of behaving within a culture group that are in opposition to ideal ways of behaving in the majority culture (Ogbu 1995a, 1995b). Negative acculturation attitudes are individuals' attitudes regarding intercultural contact and cultural maintenance that are associated with negative outcomes such as marginalization (Berry 1987, 1995). An oppositional cultural frame of reference and negative acculturation attitudes are more likely to develop as a result of cross-cultural contact in which the minority group is subordinate or disadvantaged.

An oppositional frame of reference and negative acculturation attitudes are associated with a number of negative outcomes for individuals and groups, such as acculturative stress, which is accompanied by undesirable life-changes for the individual or a community (Berry 1987, 1995; Nwadiora and McAdoo 1996) and the development of attitudes, behaviours and speech styles that are stigmatized by the dominant group. This may be accompanied by a rejection of attitudes, behaviours and ways of speaking of the dominant culture, such that individuals will not acquire the tools necessary for success in the mainstream culture (Ogbu 1995b).

Many factors that affect acculturation outcomes will be specific to particular refugee and host populations, such as the cultural and geographical distance between the two groups involved (Kaprielian-Churchill 1996). The fact that two groups who are different come into contact creates a situation of conflict. Often there is a power imbalance, in that one group has less of the knowledge and tools needed to succeed. Also, people tend to find interactions with people who are different from themselves difficult, even aversive, and tend to prefer interactions with people who are similar (Ogbu 1995a, 1995b). The extent to which these factors contribute to the development of undesirable sets of circumstances, such as the development of oppositional cultural frames of reference and acculturation attitudes and strategies associated with less adaptive outcomes, will depend on the specific characteristics of the groups in a given culture-contact situation, and the specific circumstances around this culture contact. How all these factors interact to determine developmental outcomes of groups and individuals in culture-contact situations will be discussed in more detail in the following section.

The task of acculturation

Two different theoretical perspectives, briefly outlined above, describe the task faced by people in culture-contact situations. In each case the task for individuals as they acculturate is to acquire those tools of the host culture needed to function successfully within it. Specifically, individuals must acquire 'cultural competence' sufficiently to enable them to '...carry out productive work and interact effectively with other individuals to achieve valued ends' (Gardner 1995: 228). Aspects of culture to be mastered exist in three domains: the physical world, the world of man-made artefacts and the social world. Intellectual competencies of particular importance include the acquisition of the particular symbol system used, which includes formal language, but also, for example, dance, art and rituals (Gardner 1995). Associated with this are meanings, values and goals. Children need this knowledge to be able to adapt to and function sufficiently within cultural institutions such as schools to gain access to culturally valued knowledge and expertise (Berry 1987, 1995).

The anthropological approach (Ogbu 1995b, 1995c) focuses on group-level processes that affect the accomplishment of this task. On a group level, the task for the acculturating population is to interpret the situation such that it allows members of the group to acquire the tools of the host culture, in work and education, enabling them to be successful and independent participants in the mainstream culture's activities without compromising their own cultural identity. The development of an oppositional frame of cultural reference will compromise the ability of individuals to acquire the tools of the mainstream culture while retaining group membership status. How the culture contact will be interpreted by the acculturating group depends largely on the voluntariness of the contact. Involuntary cultural minorities are at risk for developing an oppositional frame of reference as they are often also subordinate and disadvantaged compared to the mainstream culture. The impact of their collective problem of a low status may force the group to seek collective solutions, which will foster the development of strong in-group identities. Between-group differences then become markers of group membership and collective identity. Under these circumstances it becomes very difficult for individual minority group members to cross the cultural boundaries. To acquire tools, attitudes and values of the mainstream culture, including its language, means to lose their own cultural identity. Individuals who do so may experience anxiety and opposition from other members of their minority group. Ultimately the consequence might be to lose group membership and their own cultural identity (Ogbu 1995a, 1995b).

On the other hand, cultural minorities who may be just as different from the mainstream culture but who are voluntarily in the cross-cultural contact situation are likely to have different attitudes. They are likely to see the between-group differences as barriers to overcome. The acquisition of the majority culture's tools, norms and values for the purpose of upward mobility and success within the mainstream culture does not threaten their group membership or cultural identity. Members of such groups are free (and often encouraged by their peers) to acquire the ways of the mainstream culture without fear of losing their 'in-group' membership, or their own cultural identity. It is in these terms that Ogbu explains different outcomes for different cultural minorities, as evident in the United States, for example, where Asian immigrants tend to adapt successfully, and yet black Americans still suffer from the long-term trans-generational group effects of an oppositional cultural identity (Ogbu 1995a, 1995b).

There is, however, also considerable individual variability within acculturating groups (Cole 1996). Not all members of an acculturating group change to the same extent, or even in the same direction. It is the variability between individuals that is, primarily, the focus of the psychology of acculturation. Berry (1987, 1995, and 2001) identified two prime issues that concern people in culture-contact situations: firstly, *cultural maintenance* (the extent to which a group or individuals value and want to maintain their own cultural identity and the associated behaviours) and secondly, *contact participation* (the extent to which a group or individuals seek out contact with members from other cultural groups and want to participate in the everyday activities of the larger, mainstream society). Considering these two issues as independent dimensions that interact gives a grid that defines distinct acculturation strategies. These strategies carry different names depending on whether it is the minority culture or the host or mainstream culture that is considered, as illustrated in Figure 5.1.

Figure 5.1 illustrates how maintenance of heritage and cultural identity on the one hand, and relationships sought among groups on the other, predict the development of different types of acculturation strategies in the ethnocultural groups and in the larger or dominant society. Some acculturation strategies are more adaptive and associated with less stress and more desirable behavioural outcomes for individuals than others. Each is predicted by a different set of circumstances. Assimilation is the likely path of acculturation in a situation where the acculturating individual does not wish to retain their culture of origin and seeks frequent interaction with the host culture. Outcomes associated with assimilation are the acquisition of

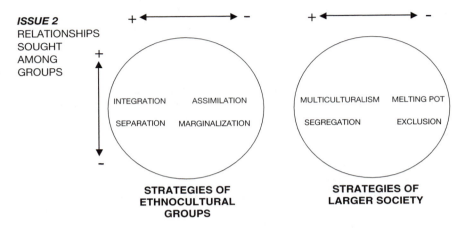

Figure 5.1 **Varieties of intercultural strategies in immigrant groups and in the receiving society** (Berry, 2001).

the norms, language and values of the host culture accompanied by the loss of the culture of origin. The converse of assimilation is separation, pre-dicted by a situation where the acculturating individual wishes to hold on to his or her own cultural values and norms and at the same time avoids con-tact with the host culture. In this scenario individuals are unlikely to acquire the tools (language, values and ways of doing things) needed to function fully in the host culture, but maintain their own cultural identity. Integration is likely when an individual wishes to do both: to hold on to his or her own culture and acquire the values, norms and tools associated with the host culture. This is considered to be the most adaptive option associ-ated with the most positive outcomes for individuals. The tools and values of the host culture are acquired additively; that is without loss of the native culture (Cole 1996; Kanal and Adrienne 1997). The least adaptive option is *marginalization*, which occurs when individuals neither maintain their cul-ture of origin, nor acquire the host culture. This is often associated with the lack of any fully functional language competency. Marginalization is a likely outcome when individuals have negative attitudes to their own cul-ture of origin as well as to the dominant culture. This is likely for individuals in groups with an oppositional frame of cultural reference. Members of such groups may reject their own culture, because of the nega-tive perceptions of it in the dominant culture, without being able to acquire the tools and values of the dominant culture. This may explain some of the difficulties experienced by members of certain minority cultures such as black Americans (Mickelson 1993; Ogbu 1995b) and Maori in New Zealand (Bishop and Glynn 1998), for example.

Acculturation is essentially a developmental phenomenon involving change within an individual over time. It is bi-directional, and both the acculturating individual and the host culture change, though usually there is one dominant culture and it is individuals of the non-dominant culture who experience the bulk of the changes. Further, acculturation may be uneven over domains; that is, individuals may seek assimilation economically (for example, in work), while remaining separate in other domains, such as religious affiliation, or parenting practices (Berry 1987, 1995). Finally, as suggested in Chapter 3, the acquisition and development of appropriate language skills may be dramatically influenced by the nature of the acculturation process.

More recently Berry (1999) also considered the level at which intercultural orientations are sought, both for the acculturating group and for the host group. As shown in Table 5.1, he argues that it is important to consider intercultural orientations at three levels in each culture: the national, the individual and the institutional level. At the national level, one would consider policies around multicultural and immigration issues in the mainstream society and group goals for the non-dominant group. At the individual level, one would consider the general multicultural ideology that exists within the dominant society and how this is associated with attitudes of individuals towards members of the non-dominant group, such as the degree of tolerance or prejudice. For the individual member of non-dominant groups this corresponds to the acculturation strategies pursued, and the extent to which culture contact and maintenance of their own cultural identity is pursued.

It is at the institutional level that conflict is most likely to arise. The most common situation is that the non-dominant group seeks equity and an appreciation of diversity, which corresponds to the integration strategy of seeking culture contact without losing the culture of origin. Institutions of the dominant culture, however, including schools, commonly prefer uniform programmes and standards, which corresponds to an assimilation approach. The role of institutions, such as those in education but also in

Table 5.1 Three levels of use of strategies (Berry 1999)

Levels	Dominant	Non-dominant
	Mainstream	Minority group
	Larger society	Cultural group
National	National politics	Group goals
Individual	Multicultural ideology	Acculturation strategies
Institutional	Uniform or plural	Diversity and equity

health and justice, for example, is therefore critical in relation to the process of acculturation and the mutual accommodation and adaptation of two groups in a culture contact situation.

Extension to Berry's model

Bourhis and colleagues (Bourhis *et al.* 1997; Perreault and Bourhis 1999) extended and modified Berry's model by considering two possible outcomes in those cases where individuals have negative attitudes towards their own as well as the host culture. The first possibility is 'anomia', defined as 'without norms', which is a highly undesirable outcome. Behavioural correlates of 'anomia' include an increased likelihood for non-conforming behaviour, such as criminality, suicidality, drug-addiction, a high divorce rate, radical political beliefs, increased rates of industrial disputes, vandalism and a low work-morale. The second possible outcome for this quadrant is that of individualization, and is more likely for members of cultures with individualistic ideologies, where people see themselves as individuals first, rather than as members of groups. Behavioural correlates of this option depend largely on characteristics of the individual. The host group's corresponding label for the individual's strategy of 'anomia' is 'exclusion'. According to Bourhis *et al.*, in circumstances where the host culture has negative attitudes both to the acculturating group's own cultural identity as well as to the acculturating group's efforts to adopt the host culture's identity, the resulting likely outcomes are either exclusion or individualization.

Finally, Bourhis *et al.* have superimposed both grids, those describing acculturation strategies of the minority culture and of the dominant group, one upon the other, to predict acculturation outcomes considering both sets of attitudes. As can be seen in Table 5.2, only 3 out of 25 possible combinations are entirely without conflict. These conditions are where both groups agree in favouring integration, or assimilation, or individualization. In situations where the host culture favours segregation or exclusion, conflict is certain, no matter what the attitude of the acculturating individuals. Where the acculturating group favours separation, conflict is only avoidable if the host culture values individualization.

Taken together, the models outlined above describe important aspects of the task the refugees need to accomplish when they arrive in a new place, namely to adapt successfully to the host society and acquire sufficient cultural competence to be able to lead productive lives. The models describe the process in terms of the dynamics inherent in the culture-contact situation. They also describe the process in terms of identifying individual and group-level factors in both the acculturating group and in the host culture. According to the model of Bourhis *et al.* (1997) the most desirable outcomes from this process are integration and multiculturalism. This means that the acculturating group or individuals are able to maintain their own

Table 5.2 Interactive acculturation model and its social consequences (according to Bourhis et al. 1997)

Host community: Low-medium, high vitality group	Immigrant community: low, medium vitality groups				
	Integration	*Assimilation*	*Separation*	*Anomia*	*Individualism*
Integration (Multiculturalism)	*Consensual*	Problematic	Conflictual	Problematic	Problematic
Assimilation (Melting Pot)	Problematic	*Consensual*	Conflictual	Problematic	Problematic
Segregation	Conflictual	Conflicted	Conflictual	Conflictual	Conflictual
Exclusion	Conflictual	Conflicted	Conflictual	Conflictual	Conflictual
Individualism	Problematic	Problematic	Problematic	Problematic	*Consensual*

Source: Richard Y. Bourhis et al., 'Towards an Interactive Acculturation Model: A Social Psychological Approach', International Journal of Psychology, 32 (6) (1997). Reprinted by permission of The International Union of Psychological Science.

positive cultural identity and maintain valued practices, while at the same time adopting those practices and ways of the dominant culture required for leading productive and happy lives in the new place. It means the host culture develops a positive multicultural ideology characterized by respect for diversity, tolerance and institutional structures that consider cultural diversity and create culturally safe environments. These outcomes are predicted in a situation where both groups in the culture-contact situation have positive attitudes to their culture and to the other cultural groups, and seek contact with each other.

There are two other outcomes which are not associated with ongoing conflict: assimilation, which requires the minority group members to actively relinquish their own cultural heritage and adopt the culture of the dominant group; and individualization, where people do not identify themselves in terms of group membership. Individualism requires both groups in the culture-contact situation to value individuality highly. This is a relatively positive outcome for individuals in situations where the dominant culture is low on multicultural ideology and relatively intolerant.

Pre-migration factors: task of acculturation

The main factor that will significantly affect the task of acculturation as described above is the voluntariness of the migration. This has been well documented, not only on a population level, but also for individuals (Berry 1987, 1995; Cushner 1998b; Kaprielian-Churchill 1996; Ogbu 1995b). Indeed, some suggest that the problems black Americans experience today are to some extent a legacy of their forced migration (Cushner 1998b). Not only are groups of involuntary migrants at risk for developing an oppositional frame of reference as described by Ogbu, but as individuals they are also at risk for developing negative attitudes to the host culture, and their own culture. Whether or not migrants view their own culture of origin positively may also depend in part on pre-migration factors, such as specific experiences, or the degree of traditionalism present in their own culture. Depending on the reasons for their forced migration, the circumstance of their flight and their trans-migration experiences, they might already view their own culture negatively. They also might already have been members of minority groups in their place of origin.

Post-migration factors: task of acculturation

The factors encountered by refugees as they arrive in the new place also influence the way acculturation occurs in groups and individuals. These include factors such as the attitudes towards migrants in the host country, the degree to which migrants are enabled to participate in the activities of the dominant culture, and the extent to which they are encouraged to maintain their own culture. Pluralistic societies, which value diversity and equity, and practice tolerance, are more likely to foster the maintenance of positive attitudes by immigrants to their culture of origin. The extent to which immigrants are able to maintain their own cultural identity will also depend on the extent to which they are permitted or encouraged to engage in cultural practices, and form associations with other members of their own ethnic group. Overt acts of discrimination are associated with the greatest impact on both the migrants and the host culture (ibid.).

The extent to which migrants will seek contact with the dominant culture will also depend on a number of factors encountered in the new place. If they encounter hostility and prejudice, for example, chances are that migrants will view the host culture more negatively than if they are met with tolerance and invited to participate fully in life in the host nation. Berry (2001) suggests that ethnic prejudice is universal. All cultural groups and all individuals have some level of prejudice about other groups. Prejudice is very variable across groups and individuals, though. How tolerant individuals and groups are able to be towards others depends to some extent on how secure they are in their own cultural identity. According to Berry, only people who are secure in their own cultural identity will be tolerant of others who are different (Berry 2001).

Schools are one of the prime acculturating agents within societies. It is here that the values, norms and tools of a particular culture are transmitted to its young. This includes the multicultural ideology of the dominant group as well as attitudes and beliefs about specific migrant groups. Furthermore, the values, norms and goals of the dominant society will be reflected in the practices of institutions such as schools. Ogbu (1995b) argues that in many schools, multicultural education is not about raising the academic achievement levels of minority group children, but rather that the primary goals are social integration, citizenship, and raising self-esteem.

To some extent all children, when they first start school, have to adapt to a new culture – that of the school. All children in all cultures acquire their cultures in terms of what it takes to get ahead, their language, and so on; how they do this differs from one culture to another, but it also differs from how learning happens at school. When children go to school they are expected to learn what the school teaches (the curriculum) and also how to learn – that is, the learning style of 'school'. All children have to adapt and manage this transition, including the children of the mainstream culture. How well children adapt to school depends on how similar, or different, their cultural frames of reference are, or if they are oppositional (Ogbu 1995b). An example of similar groups in culture contact would be white middle-class British migrating to the United States. Examples of very different groups in culture contact would be Asians who migrated to the United States for the purpose of economic advancement. Many Asian migrants to the United States adapt very well, in spite of being very different. An example of oppositional groups in culture contact include members of the hippy movement in the 1960s in the United States, or black Americans, who have developed strong in-group identities which are in conflict with the goals and values of the mainstream society (ibid.). Many members of such groups, even though they are born in the 'host country' and have its language as their native tongue, do not succeed in the schools of the dominant culture because of their oppositional frame of cultural reference, which rejects the goals, values and tools of the mainstream culture.

Schools are also a prime point of contact between new immigrants and the host culture. As such they are ideally situated to promote positive cross-cultural experiences for individual students as well as implement interventions which foster the development of positive acculturation attitudes in refugees and positive multicultural ideologies in all students.

Other individual factors that affect the acculturation of young migrants specifically have been identified in the research literature. Hyman *et al.* (2000), for example, found that among Asian refugees in Toronto the different rates of acculturation within families were often associated with conflict. The differential rates of language acquisition, for example, or differences in the degree to which children and young people wish to adopt the ways of the dominant culture can lead to intergenerational conflict in the homes of refugees. This often leads to a situation where children hardly even speak to their own parents and are isolated within their own families.

Problems with school adjustment, however, were also common among this group of refugees. Many of the young people studied felt marginalized, which they often attributed to a lack of language competency. Culture conflict due to large differences in expectations around how to behave in schools was also a major issue. For example, in Vietnamese schools it is not considered appropriate to ask for help, or to answer questions with 'I don't know' (ibid.). The authors of that study made a number of practical recommendations including the need to recognize the multiple stresses experienced by acculturating youths; the need for orientation programmes to help families identify competing familial and societal values, and to encourage parental involvement in schools; the need for respecting traditional values of migrants on one hand while facilitating the acquisition of tools needed to succeed in the host culture on the other hand; and, finally, to eradicate cultural stereotypes.

Another study that examined acculturation of Vietnamese refugees in the United States (Chung *et al.* 2000) found that the age of the child at the time of migration affected the ease of acculturation. Younger children had fewer problems. Migration during adolescence, on the other hand, when social and cultural identities are critical, may be particularly problematic. Gender effects were also observed. There were large gender differences in the cohort that migrated when they were older in the extent to which the young men and women had acculturated. The women showed larger acculturation effects. The authors argued that for older girls, who had already developed a cultural identity, adopting western gender roles was advantageous, since this was associated with more autonomy. The young men on the other hand stood to lose status and were, therefore, slower to acculturate and relinquish their traditional gender roles (ibid.).

Post-migration: facilitating positive acculturation outcomes

Much can be done to ease the task of acculturation and to facilitate positive outcomes for refugees. Some potential interventions have already been identified above.

Of particular interest are the points of contact between the acculturating individual and the host culture – wherever they occur. It is in the interactions between them, at any level, that tensions lie. It is here, therefore, that solutions need to be sought. However, it is suggested that to be effective, change needs to occur at a systems level, with the goal of conflict resolution by removing the barriers erected for the individual by society (Cushner 1998b; Emminghaus 1987). This is considered the only 'causal' approach and involves interventions aimed at the policy level and the institutions within a society (including schools). This approach is supported by Bronfenbrenner's ecological model (1992), which describes the interconnectedness of the social environment from a systems level down to the immediate environment surrounding individuals. A compensatory approach is directed at the administration within a country in terms of the application of the law for example, as it affects refugees, but also at the interpersonal level where positive intercultural encounters can be fostered by providing information and encouraging communication, thereby reducing misunderstanding. Interventions aimed at individuals are described by Emminghaus as 'props'. These are the kinds of interventions which teach individuals tolerance or coping skills (Emminghaus 1987).

Schools are important sites for both long-term and short-term interventions at several levels. Cushner (1998b) suggests that a potential long-term goal of education could be to prepare the minds of all young people to include a diversity of viewpoints, behaviours and values, thus preparing them for life in multicultural societies. More immediately, effective schools need to implement strategies and programmes designed to remove the cultural barriers as much as possible. To achieve this, in-service teacher education may be required as many teachers are currently 'ill-prepared for the diversity in their classrooms' (Cole 1996; Cushner 1998b: 361). Safe multicultural schools are characterized by the setting of high learning standards and clear behavioural expectations as well as the promotion of cooperative climates, all within interdisciplinary school-based programmes with an overall ecological orientation (Cole 1996). This means that problems are not seen as belonging to the student, but as a result of poor interactions between students and their environment. With this approach, the multiple needs of children such as refugees can be catered for with the aim of preventing negative outcomes (ibid.). Such ecological approaches will do much to prevent the development of barriers, particularly in educational contexts, that arise from treating people who are different, including refugees, as people with deficiencies in need of remediation (Bishop and Glynn 1998; Kanal and Adrienne 1997).

Cushner (1998b), in a conclusion to an edited book about multicultural education, summarizes the responses of the various authors to a scenario he set at the outset of the book. The authors, given the scenario of a large number of refugees suddenly entering their countries, were asked what they thought should be done.

Though Cushner accepts that the answers are somewhat idealized, there are similarities which, taken together, reflect the thinking of a number of leading experts in the field today. These are some of the recommendations made:

- Most nations suggested that refugees need some support on arrival (health care, help with finding employment, access to counselling services and interpreters, and language training).
- Most recommended that all parties should be involved in the design and delivery of programmes and services. Refugee populations should be consulted and represented on school committees as soon as possible.
- Maintenance of language of origin should be fostered, through the use of bilingual teachers, in addition to ESL provisions.
- Though a host of other services and agencies may need to be involved, schools were seen as the central settings, where various communities could come together.
- Teacher training in issues related to diversity was seen as essential.
- Pluralism was seen as an overall goal, avoiding assimilationist ideologies.

In conclusion, Cushner cites Banks (1993) who suggests that: 'The major goal of multicultural education is to restructure schools so that all students will acquire the knowledge, attitudes, and skills needed to function in an ethnically diverse nation and world' (Cushner 1998a). Cushner's thinking, and the recommendations of a number of educationists that he had summarized, is in accord with recommendations that arise from the acculturation theories and with issues identified arising from the process of displacement, that are described in this chapter.

What happens as a result of cross-cultural contact depends largely, as argued above, on the nature of the cultures which meet and the circumstances under which they come into contact. Potential outcomes range from an acculturation experience that is positive and enriching for both cultures involved, to outcomes that lead to the development of transgenerational cycles of disadvantage in the acculturating group, an outcome which in the long run represents an economic and social burden for all (Cole 1996). In between, there is a spectrum of degrees of stress experienced by individuals, and variation in the degree to which they successfully negotiate cultural adaptation to the new society and become full participants in its activities. Children who are able to maintain biculturality perform better at school (ibid.). Promoting biculturality requires an ecological approach involving the provision of multilingual services for students and their families and staff development to improve the interactions between acculturating children and the host culture (Beiser *et al.* 1995). Such an approach will also be better able to cater for the within-group diversity in groups of refugee children (Cole 1996).

Conclusion

The potential negative outcomes of unsuccessful acculturation by any groups are far reaching and very difficult to remediate, as can be seen by the problems still experienced many generations later in black Americans, for example. These kinds of outcomes are largely avoidable, but this requires significant change of attitude at a population, policy and institutional level. The ecological model developed in Chapter 1 of this book is particularly relevant in the description of issues arising out of the process of migration in terms of displacement and acculturation. The processes that determine outcomes are affected by factors on the systems, institutional and individual levels in both groups. Preventative initiatives aimed at minimizing the risk of negative outcomes that result from the process of migration need to target all levels. Tolerance and respect for cultural diversity need to be evident at the policy level, in a country's institutions, and in the attitudes of the general population. A nation-wide policy to foster the development of positive multicultural attitudes in schools, formalized in the curriculum, would represent such an initiative.

Chapter 6

Schools, teachers and education of refugee children

Richard Hamilton

One of the major tasks facing the refugee child when arriving in a new country is to adapt to a new school environment. In coming to grips with this task, the child brings many pre-migration, trans-migration and post-migration characteristics and experiences that have the potential to facilitate or interfere; for example, the nature of the flight and the refugee experience, level of literacy in first language, and parental support. One set of post-migration variables that will critically influence the child's adaptation process resides within the school, namely the characteristics of schools and teachers. It is important to emphasize that not only will the refugee child be required to adapt but schools, teachers and existing students will also need to adapt. To know how best to prepare teachers to meet the needs of refugee children and how to create schools that can meet these needs is crucial.

In adopting an ecological view of the refugee child's development and learning, it is hoped that we can better understand how to help schools and teachers prepare themselves as well as how best to facilitate the involvement of refugee students and families within schools. For all children, schools fulfil the function of focusing other related systems (for example, families and community services) on the task of facilitating children's development in order to prepare the child to contribute to the wider society. As indicated in earlier chapters, the ecological systems view of child development (Bronfenbrenner 1993) assumes that the child both influences and is influenced by his or her natural environment. Bronfenbrenner identified a variety of layered systems that directly or indirectly influenced the child's development; for example, schools, community, family, helping services and society. The child is at the centre of and embedded within these layered systems which interact with each other and with the child to influence development in very important ways.

The main purpose of this chapter is to summarize the general literature on school and teacher effects, to look specifically at these effects within the refugee education context, and, finally, to identify implications for better preparing schools and teachers for teaching refugee children.

School and teacher effects

There has been much research that has looked at how the structure and characteristics of schools influence the nature of classrooms and interactions between teachers and students (Fuller and Clarke 1994; Jansen 1995; Waxman and Walberg 1991). Research on effective schools has a long and varied history. It is currently going through major debates concerning the paradigms underlying current research and the techniques employed to assess school effectiveness (Jansen 1995; Scheemers *et al.* 2000; Teddlie and Reynolds 2000). An approach often employed within this area is to select unusually 'effective' schools and identify how they differ from other schools. An effective school is defined as one that consists of students who demonstrate particular positive behaviours (one or more) at rates higher than one would predict given the student, family and community characteristics (Good and Weinstein 1986). The student behaviours include high scores on standardized tests, good school attendance, low rates of disruptive classroom behaviour or delinquency, a high rate of post-secondary school attendance and high self-esteem.

The following characteristics have been associated with 'effective' schools: strong leadership by the principal which creates a commitment to excellence; a safe school environment; teachers who possess positive attitudes and expectations concerning all students' ability to achieve; effective use of instructional time and emphasis on the importance of mastery; comprehensive monitoring of student progress and acquisition of skills; and high levels of parental involvement (Creemers and Scheerens 1989; Fan and Chen 2001; Reynolds and Teddlie 2000; Stringfield and Herman,1996; Teddlie and Stringfield 1993). All of these characteristics of effective schools are important within the context of refugee education; however, there are four that are particularly salient and will be discussed further, namely the role of principals, parental involvement, teacher expectations and school environment.

Principal involvement and leadership

The literature on effective schools consistently finds that the most effective are those which include a principal who is an active leader and who supports the teaching efforts of teachers (Sergiovanni 1994). In particular, when schools are adopting alternative approaches to teaching or implementing a new curriculum (such as a programme for teaching refugee students), Waugh (1994) suggests that principals and administrators play a critical part. Unless teachers are receptive to the changes required within new curricula or the adoption or use of new approaches, the new curricula and programmes will fail to be implemented as intended within the classroom. A complex number of factors is likely to affect teacher reactions towards a new curriculum or teaching approach. Those reactions, in turn, will influence subsequent implementation and maintenance efforts. Hall and Hord (1987), in their concerns based adoption model (CBAM), suggest that change is a developmental process and that individuals will experience different concerns at various stages of project implementation. Research has found that teachers vary widely in their adoption and implementation of new approaches and curricula (Fullan and Pomfret 1977; Molman *et al.* 1982; Waugh and Punch 1987). Many researchers have focused on the significant impact of the target community and institutions on the implementation process (Berman and McLaughlin 1980; Roberts-Gray 1985). One critical influence on this process is the leadership role played by principals and administrators in supporting the use and implementation of a new approach or curriculum.

To ensure that teachers are receptive to new approaches, principals and administrators need to engage in a variety of supportive and promoting activities (Waugh and Godfrey 1995). First of all, principals need to emphasize the benefits of implementing or taking advantage of the new approach or available services. Secondly, they need to allow and offer support to teachers to tailor the new approach to their specific classroom, teaching styles and content. Principals who can find some extra time for teachers to plan and communicate with peers will be providing some of the necessary conditions for expanding teacher's roles and, consequently, improving student learning. Thirdly, principals need to create a mechanism that allows teachers to express their concerns about the new programme or initiative and have those concerns answered. The way school resources are employed and the way teachers are encouraged to interact with one another have a direct influence on the effectiveness of a school (Brophy 1985; Rosentholtz 1989; Sizer 1992). Fourthly, they need to include teachers in decision-making regarding how best to implement programmes and programmatic changes within their classrooms. Schools where teachers engage in considerable job-related discussion and share in decisions about instructional programmes and staff development are more effective than schools where decisions are made by hard and fast procedures and rules (Barth 1990; Schlechty and Vance 1983). Finally, principals need to support publicly the new programme or initiative, at least by identifying and presenting the advantages of the initiative or opportunity.

Within the context of refugee education, the principal can play a vital role in leading and supporting teacher development and in the use of new techniques which are particularly useful in helping refugee students adapt to a new school environment. The principal, in essence, also acts as a gatekeeper and facilitator for the use and integration of community and agency helping services, which can serve an invaluable role within the refugee education context.

Parental involvement

Parental involvement in education has been found to have a positive influence on student performance and behaviour in schools (Fan and Chen 2001; Keith *et al.* 1986; Lee *et al.* 1993; Raywid 1985). A variety of parental behaviours, from monitoring children's homework and creating a quiet place to do homework to volunteering in their children's schools and classroom, has been found to relate positively to student academic performance (Henderson 1987). In addition, secondary schools which foster positive parent–school interactions have been found to be more effective schools (Chubb and Moe 1990). That is, parents of children in 'effective' secondary schools visited classrooms, were involved in school activities and had regular meetings with teachers.

Lee *et al.* (1993) suggested that attempts to increase parental involvement in schools typically involved one or more of the following strategies: parent education programmes; functional communities around the school; and community control. Parental education programmes which have focused on training parents to become better home educators and to engage in supportive academic behaviours have produced positive effects on student performance (for example, Becker 1984). Developing functional communities around the schools involves creating mechanisms which invite and encourage parents and members from the relevant cultural community into the activities of the school. This requires that schools adopt an outreach mentality and view themselves as a potential centre for community action and activities. Finally, the community control approach advocates that parents gain some control of schools and their administration, with control ranging from parents becoming responsible for school site management to parent–school partnerships. This approach is often employed when those individuals running the schools are seen to be insensitive to local community needs. Such a mismatch between community needs and school climate and environment can be due to a variety of factors, such as federal educational policy or the entrenched interests of those managing the school (Lee *et al.* 1993).

In order to increase refugee parental involvement in schools, schools need to develop parental education programmes and outreach programmes. Schools need to help parents develop skills (for example, second language skills) which will allow them to participate more fully in their child's education experience, and to support the efforts of schools. In particular, parents will need support in understanding the curriculum and how to help their children choose topics as, in other cultures, parents and children are often not given such choices. In addition, schools need to develop functional communities that integrate services and members from the target cultural community to support the education of refugee children.

Teacher attitudes and expectations

Although there is some controversy over the direct effects of teacher expectation on student achievement and development (Jussim *et al.* 1998; Spitz 1999), there is clear evidence that teacher expectations influence teacher behaviours within the classroom and their interactions with students (Dusek 1985; Smith and Sheppard 1988; Weinstein and McKown 1998). That is, teachers have been shown to moderate their interactions with students based on their expectations for different levels of achievement or performance (Ennis 1998). This is important, for differential teacher behaviour has been found to be related to differences in student performance and classroom environments (Brophy 1985). Consequently, in the worst possible instance, teacher behaviours may create a negative snowball effect by virtue of their reactions and feedback to students.

Of interest in the context of refugee education is the evidence that individual differences among teachers and also among students moderate expectancy effects (ibid.). In particular, research has found that teachers who hold rigid stereotypes and social class biases and who tend to differentiate between high and low achieving students are more likely to produce negative expectation effects (Snow *et al.* 1996). Given that refugees often come from very different cultures and possess different values and goals from those held by members of the country within which they are settling, the potential for conflicting stereotypes or biases to enter into teacher–student interactions is heightened. Consequently, initiatives that are aimed at influencing teacher views, knowledge and expectations related to the culture of the incoming refugee students need to be part of any attempt to have a significant impact on refugee education.

Safe school environment

Unless schools are safe environments in which children can flourish without being victimized, taunted, bullied, or at worst, physically harmed, then the children will be seriously hampered in their attempts to learn and develop. As is evident from recent incidents, particularly in the United States, schools are becoming increasingly unsafe (Nolin 1996; Pelligrini 2002). Bullying is now recognised as a serious problem in many educational systems throughout the world. Estimates indicate that 30 per cent or more of students have either been the victim of a bully or have been a bully at some point in their schooling (Snow *et al.* 1996). According to Olweus (1998), who has done research on bullying in the United States, Scandinavia and other European countries, most bullying occurs at school, rather than on the way to or from school. Teachers usually do little to stop it and most parents are unaware of it. Some researchers have found that well-designed bullying prevention programmes can reduce, prevent and eliminate bullying (Olweus and Limber

1999; Peterson and Skiba 2000). According to Peterson and Skiba (2000) and Pelligrini (2002), effective bullying prevention programmes include the development of whole-school policy and its integrated implementation. School staff, parents and students must be made aware of the extent, nature and consequences of bullying within their school, and must be involved in the analysis of the problem and the development and application of a school-wide intervention programme aimed at reducing bullying (compare with Roland 2000). Successful whole-school interventions must also include a peer-level component which teaches specific skills, for example, social skills, and encourages students to share their concerns over being bullied (Eslea and Smith, 1998; Pelligrini 2002).

One of the critical determinants of whether an individual student will be the target of bullying or inappropriate treatment is likely to be the degree to which the student conforms to the prevailing norms or values of the majority culture. In the case of integrating refugee students into schools, there is a high potential for the refugees to be the target of bullying and racism. Schools need to adopt strict policies, procedures and monitoring systems in order to ensure that refugees are not subject to bullying and racism.

Teacher effects, school effects and refugee education

Facilitating refugee children's adaptation into a new and foreign school system is a complicated process that requires interventions at multiple levels. How a school is organized, its relationship with parents and community, and how teachers interact and instruct students are all factors that will dramatically influence the success of students in general, and refugee children in particular.

Schools need to develop specific policies and procedures that focus on ensuring the creation of a mutually adaptive relationship between the refugee child, his or her parents, schools, and surrounding community and helping services (Brizuela and Garcia-Sellers 1999). These policies and procedures should promote and support the development of clear communication channels between the school and home; parental participation in school activities and the child's education; host country students' awareness of the refugee community and culture; teacher understanding and support for the needs and interests of the child, family, and culture; a safe school environment free from racism and bullying; and the integrated use of multiple service providers (Bolloten and Spafford 1998; Hyder 1998; Jones 1998; Jupp and Luckey 1990; Leiper de Monchy 1991; Lodge 1998; Ready 1991; Richman 1998; Rutter 1994; Sherriff 1995; Wagner and Lodge 1995).

One could argue that it would be important for all schools to have these characteristics; however, within the context of refugee education, the above-mentioned areas are crucial to ensuring a safe environment for these children as well as increasing these students' learning and self-esteem. It is the special circumstances that surround the children's participation and presence here that create complex and sensitive issues requiring well-developed policies as well as further teacher development and change.

The following section reviews in more detail the research on characteristics required for schools to support the education of refugee children effectively.

Home–school communication channels

The importance of clear and open communication between schools and homes cannot be overestimated. One way to open up communication between the child, school and parents is through a mediator. Mediators, who need to have an in-depth understanding of both the culture of the school and that of the refugee family and child, can act as brokers to develop good communication channels between the child, school and parents. Although the mediator can be thought of as an individual, there is no reason to suppose that an organization or set of individuals could not play this vital role.

Several researchers have shown the importance of communication and the positive role that can be played by a mediator. Brizuela and Garcia-Sellers (1999) found that mediation plays an important role in facilitating the child's transition from one culture to the other by helping to develop common perspectives and an area of overlap between home and school. Richman (1998) highlights the importance of connecting parents and children with a mediator from the beginning of their involvement in schools. Multiple meetings with parents within the first two or three months of the child's entry into the school are considered critical to building a safe and comfortable relationship with parents. Bolloten and Spafford (1998), in their description of approaches to supporting refugee children in East London primary schools, identify the value of a 'refugee support teacher' who, in addition to other duties, facilitates communication between teachers, schools, parents and children.

Kelly and Bennoun (1984) and Jupp and Luckey (1990), in their research on the experience of Indochinese refugees in Australia, found that students and their parents felt unprepared for the education system. They also found that the poor communication and exchange of information between parents and schools contributed significantly to the children's poor performance in school. These results are echoed by Stead *et al.* (1999) in their research on Kosova refugees in Scotland.

Within New Zealand, Humpage (1998) found that for Somali refugee adolescents, the lack of parent–school communication was a major obstacle in resolving other refugee–student related difficulties. Sherriff (1995) surveyed parents and refugee community organizations involved in meeting the needs of refugee children from the Horn of Africa who were brought to Great Britain. One of the major issues that influenced the quality of the education of those children was the need for effective communication between parents and schools. Jones (1998), in a summary of a case study of a primary school in Greenwich, England, found that a lack of communication between the school and parents was a significant barrier to the children's adequate progress and education. Finally, Richman (1998) and Sherriff (1995) emphasize the importance of creating mechanisms that will support parents' acquisition of the host language by, for example, organizing language classes at the school and creating babysitting opportunities for mothers of young children in order for them to attend existing classes.

One of the critical mechanisms for setting the tone for communication between parents and schools is the induction process. Pollard and Filer (1996) in their case studies of schools within Great Britain, found the way in which refugee children and families were welcomed into the school significantly affected the initial progress of the child, and the capacity of the family to provide help.

A good induction process is a two-way interchange between the school and the parents and children which includes gathering information about the child and parents; describing school policies and procedures; and encouraging parents to become involved in the school (Richman 1998). In addition, the induction process should introduce mechanisms which should ease the child's and parents' transition into the school; that is, assign a buddy to the refugee child and introduce a liaison person as a contact person (ibid.). Finally, the induction process should include a basic social and educational assessment administered by a bicultural worker (Richman 1998; van Hees 1994).

According to Richman (1998) and van Hees (1994), social assessments should at minimum include gathering information about who lives with the child, details of moves and changes of caretakers, social familial network, refugee status, housing situation and health problems. The basic educational assessment should include gathering information on languages spoken at home, the child's previous education and achievements, the child's current English language abilities, the parents' education and language literacy and the amount of academic support available from home.

One of the benefits of clear communication between parents and schools is that it may help overcome potential mismatches between prior conceptions, values and goals of schools and parents. A refugee entering into a new school system is not only entering a new educational environment but is also entering a new cultural environment which may be aligned with different values and goals (Zhou and Bankston 2000). Ogbu (1988, 1986), in his discussion of the mismatch between school and home for disadvantaged children within the United States, indicated that there was often some level of distrust and suspicion surrounding interactions between parents and the school. He indicated that often teachers described parents' actions and approaches as interfering with the educational goals of schools, while parents suggested that teachers ignored and even devalued the culture of the home.

One factor that will influence the degree to which cultural difference interferes with or facilitates refugee children's adaptation process is whether their cultural frames of reference are similar, different or in opposition to the majority cultural frames of reference (Ogbu 1995b). Cultural frames of reference define the correct or ideal way to behave within a culture (ibid.), and different or oppositional frames of reference will interfere with a child's educational adaptation process. According to Ogbu, involuntary immigrants, including refugees, are more likely to possess different cultural frames of reference, and in some instances may possess oppositional frames of reference.

Humpage (1998) found that Somali refugee students in New Zealand had very different frames of reference in terms of school behaviour, roles and values. She found tensions between values of home culture and those of the educational culture. In addition, the Somalians' lack of experience with group approaches, lack of writing skills, and difficulty with being on time interfered with appropriate educational progress. Kelly and Bennoun (1984), in their research on the experience of Indochinese refugees in Australia, observed that teachers, students and parents had quite different views of students' experiences in the education system and what they wanted from it. Rousseau *et al.* (1996) found a wide mismatch between teachers' and parents' perception of the difficulties that existed in refugees entering Canadian schools. For parents, the biggest problem was different cultural expectations between the family and schools. Teachers, on the other hand, felt that lack of language ability on the part of the parents was the main cause of the communication difficulties between home and school. It is very likely that both perceptions captured a real problem in the communicative environment between schools and parents.

Hoyt (1995) reviewed the efforts and outcomes of trying to increase parental involvement of Southeast Asian refugee children in American schools from 1987 to 1994. She suggested a variety of approaches to promote parental involvement which ranged from home–school journals, to explicitly explaining classroom goals (which may differ dramatically from typical classroom goals found in the refugee's home country) to employing a collaborative–participatory approach between parents, schools and community service providers.

In summary, the clash of cultural values and expectations that occurs when refugee children enter into schools can be eased with proactive planning focused on the development of clear communication channels, well-developed induction schemes, extensive teacher support and training, and mechanisms for community outreach and integration. Just as teachers are trained to gather as much information as they can about new native students who come into their classrooms, so they should gather as much as they can about new refugee students who come into their classrooms. The diversity that the refugee children bring to the classroom may in many cases overlap with the cultural and experiential diversity already present in the classroom. Alternatively, however, they may also bring characteristics and behaviours that are new and somewhat unsettling for teachers.

Parental involvement in schools

Creating clear communication channels with parents is reciprocally related to increasing parental involvement in schools. That is, clearer communication increases the likelihood that parents will become involved in schools, and, as parents become more involved in various school activities, communication channels are further developed and solid connections occur between the parents and the school. Consequently, the earlier discussion on the development of clear communication channels and explicit induction procedures should increase the probability that parents become more involved in schools. Increased parental involvement in schools will increase parental knowledge of and sense of comfort with the school and will offer multiple opportunities for the gathering of additional information about the parents and children (Richman 1998).

Cole (1996) suggested that school can provide multilingual opportunities to increase parent involvement in the educational life of their children. According to Cole, parents may be reluctant to approach the school if they are at a stage of settlement where they are focusing on adjustment, or they lack language skills. Consequently, schools need to reach out to refugee parents by getting them involved in volunteer programmes and first language tutoring programmes and by asking them for assistance in identifying appropriate multilingual resources. In addition, after-school activities focused on the development of English language capabilities and parental education classes on enhancing the academic progress of their children should also increase their involvement in schools. Finally, as indicated earlier, regular meetings organized and run by a mediator will go a long way to facilitating parental involvement in schools.

Lopez et al. (2001) indicated that it was critical for schools to aim to meet parental needs above all other involvement considerations. That is, depending on the target parent population, the definition of 'involvement' may differ dramatically such that it is important that schools do not adopt the same expectations for involvement for all parents within the school, irrespective of their needs. This clearly suggests that not only is it likely that refugee parents will have different involvement needs from the majority population but that parents from different refugee populations (even within the same school) may have different involvement needs.

Teacher support for child and family needs

Jones and Rutter (1998) suggest that there is a real danger that teachers will harbour some misconceptions about the impact of refugee experiences on refugee children. Research on educational provisions for students enrolled in inner city schools within London suggests that it is likely that refugees will elicit low teacher expectations (Department of Education and Science 1980). Not all refugee children are traumatized and in need of specialized help, although some may clearly require extra support (Stead *et al.* 1999). In addition, the lack of appropriate experiences and skills (for example, in the host language) should not be used as a basis on which to assume that refugee children will be at an extreme disadvantage. It is important not to develop low expectations for refugee children in terms of their academic capabilities or in terms of the nature of their future goals.

Humpage (1998) found that teacher expectations of Somali refugee students in New Zealand presented a barrier to the students becoming competent. That is, teachers labelled the refugee aspirations as unrealistic and such expectations influenced their behaviour toward the students. Sherriff (1995) found in her survey on the integration of African refugees within Great Britain that parents of Somali and Eritrean children indicated that professionals in health, social services and education had little understanding of their culture, background, lifestyles and the critical differences that existed between refugees and migrants. They were consequently unlikely to take into account the effects of being a refugee in their interactions with refugees. The most effective way to influence teacher expectations about refugee students and what it means to be a refugee is to help them to gain knowledge of the different cultures, values and beliefs of the students who are in the classroom (Bolloten and Spafford 1998).

In order for teachers to develop cross-cultural competence, they need to become aware of their own cultural beliefs and values, develop knowledge of information specific to the cultures that exist within their classroom and develop skills to engage in each culture (Hyder 1998). According to Hyder, teachers can facilitate the development of cross-cultural competence in their own students by helping the students to note the similarities and differences in how children and adults look, speak, dress and so on, and to see differences as positive and not indicative of some type of deficit. Teachers also need to adopt 'culturally-responsive teaching' approaches. Culturally-responsive teaching includes teachers acknowledging cultural diversity in classrooms, supporting this diversity in instruction by accepting and valuing differences, accommodating different learning styles and building on cultural backgrounds (Sparks 1989).

Hyder (1998) indicates that teaching values diversity is critical in the pre-school and early years of schooling because it sets the tone for both the refugee and home country students in terms of their views on cultural differences. Hyder (1998) and Clark and Millikan (1986) suggest the use of 'home corners' as an important part of any pre-school or early school context. 'Home corners' are parts of the classroom which have been designated to represent the 'home' of children within the classroom. They are useful because they can reflect a variety of homes as well as offering opportunities for children to act out situations they have experienced in places such as airports or hospitals.

Teachers may require extensive support in their attempts to foster and encourage cultural diversity within their classrooms. Given the nature of teaching and schools, there may be many instances in which teachers will be so overwhelmed with existing duties that they may not be positively disposed to learning new approaches to teaching. Humpage (1998) found that teachers in secondary schools in New Zealand possessed cultural blinkers in that they actively resisted the idea that they needed to know more about the circumstances of refugee students from Somalia. These teachers already felt it was difficult to make decisions about student needs, and introducing another variable based on the refugee experience would add to the complexity of teaching.

A safe school environment

In order to create a positive educational framework that will allow refugee children to integrate easily into a new school environment, they need to feel safe and comfortable. Richman (1998) and Wagner and Lodge (1995) indicate that the development and enforcement of clear policies on racism and bullying are critical features of a safe school environment for refugee students. In addition to integrating their experiences in the curriculum, refugee students will appreciate and value teachers who take racism seriously (Melzak and Warner 1992).

Rutter (1994), in her review of refugee education initiatives within Great Britain, summarized approaches taken by schools that were particularly effective in dealing with and preventing refugee education problems. In addition to extra academic support for students, teacher support, use of a dedicated support person, and well-developed induction policies and procedures, effective schools had a curriculum that included issues such as human rights, racism and bullying. This proactive approach was found to eliminate difficult problems and situations which arose during the integration of refugees into schools.

In addition, Cole (1996) suggests the need to build multicultural school communities which promote a multicultural perspective and address the needs of both immigrant and refugee families; that is, a multicultural curriculum, integration of multicultural community services, translation services, English language courses, and multicultural training for teachers. For many schools, transformation into a multicultural community will require multilingual services and staff professional development. Although teachers may already be very familiar with and have adopted a view which can accommodate and value individual differences within the classroom, refugee students may well stretch them far beyond their capabilities.

In order for comprehensive multicultural school-based programmes to be instituted, schools will need to adopt an ecological orientation to education (ibid.). An ecological multicultural perspective requires that schools and teachers move away from viewing any socialization or academic student problem as reflective of some underlying dysfunction on the part of the child to viewing these problems as being indicative of a poor fit between the school environment and the individual student (Moore *et al.* 1999) (see Chapter 7). The focus of interventions should be on making the school environment more suitable to the needs of the child.

Conclusion

I have taken the view that one cannot understand and, therefore, develop appropriate interventions for helping better educate refugee children if one isolates the different players within this context; that is, the child, the school, the family, the community and the service providers. Refugees arrive in a new country with a plethora of needs and require a variety of services (educational, medical, vocational) to ease their way into the new cultural environment. The focus of this chapter was primarily on the interactions between the child, teachers, schools and families. It is, however, critical to note that other systems in the sphere of the child can dramatically increase the child's comfort in adapting to the new school environment. Health providers, government support services, private refugee support services, career and vocational development services, and housing authorities all play an important part in creating a productive educational environment.

The key to developing schools which effectively educate refugee students is to create mechanisms that facilitate and foster positive and supportive interactions between the different systems (parents, teacher, schools, community and service providers), with the child as the focal point. In order for this to happen, these parties need to have a better understanding of the nature and needs of each other and methods to negotiate mutually satisfying ways of meeting needs.

In addition to the acquisition of skills for teaching potentially traumatized children, teachers need to acquire more knowledge about the different cultures represented by refugees and the refugee experiences (for example, human rights, flight, loss and displacement). Furthermore, it is clear that principals play a critical part in advancing and supporting both the development and implementation of alternative approaches to teaching refugees, as well as in the coordination and integration of the multiple service providers who contribute to the overall well-being of the refugee child. It must also be remembered that peers play an important part in creating a safe and supportive environment for refugee children; just as teachers need to expand their knowledge of different cultures, the importance of diversity within classrooms and the plight of refugees, so similar initiatives aimed at students should be developed and implemented.

Schools are also instrumental in preparing and supporting refugee parents and children to take advantage of the educational and supportive experiences and services that exist within our schools, community and society. An inability to communicate due to lack of language facility or to a clash of cultural values and beliefs has the potential to disrupt the exchange of information between schools, children, parents and service providers. Every effort must be made, therefore, to make sure that parents are able and encouraged to get involved in school activities and their child's education, and are able to take advantage of community services.

In summary, it is clear that the specific characteristics of schools, their policies and teaching practices will play an important role in ensuring the successful integration of refugee children. In terms of best practice, the policies and practices that ensure that refugee children can learn and grow within a safe and supportive environment include:

- effective communication channels between the school and home
- an explicit and clearly developed induction process
- policies for eliminating racism and bullying
- principal leadership in supporting teachers and programmes which focus on helping refugee students
- the active participation of parents within schools
- increased teacher knowledge of the refugee culture and community
- professional development of teachers aimed at increasing their skills for teaching traumatized children
- the participation of students from the host country in programmes to expand their knowledge of different cultures.

There are many potential barriers to the establishment and maintenance of schools which can effectively educate refugee children. Refugee children and their families often bring with them experiences, characteristics and patterns of behaviour which interfere with the effective education of the children; for example, the inability of parents to communicate with schools and teachers. In developing interventions aimed at facilitating the education of refugee children it is, therefore, important to include systemic and ecological mechanisms which will address any barriers to creating and maintaining an effective educational environment.

Chapter 7

Conceptual and policy issues

Dennis Moore

The primary purpose of this review has been to distil from the literature suggestions of best practice to facilitate the safe and effective inclusion of refugee students into our schools. Our brief carries a dual focus: on the one hand, a focus on refugee students and the factors which may affect their ability to adapt to their new schools and, on the other, a focus on the ecological factors which impact the school's ability to maximize the successful non-traumatic transition of the refugee into a new culture and learning environment. We have reviewed discrete but interrelated bodies of research which consider the impact of trauma and grief, language differences, resilience factors, teacher and school effects and culture on this process, and have developed a model of the interrelationships of these factors.

Two common themes in the literature are a focus on the child-in-context and a degree of concern regarding the destructive power of the deficit-model reasoning (where a child's failure to learn is attributed to a deficit in the individual child) that pervades so much of contemporary educational practice. Clearly, a range of pre-migration, personal, and post-migration factors suggest that refugee children are an identifiable group of students with special educational needs though they may not fit the conventional criteria for special education assistance (Cole 1996). In this light, instructive parallels may be drawn with deficit-model thinking in the provision of special education whereby many students from minority cultures have been excluded from participating fully in the regular classroom discourse (see President's Commission on Excellence in Special Education, 2002).

Special education: deficit or differences

Forness (1981), Moore *et al.* (1999) and others have, in reviewing the special education literature, identified two major currents which have resulted in a sea change in the resourcing and provision for special needs related to behaviour and learning in education in recent years. The first of these is a shift in values throughout the Western world toward greater equity for all, and the second is a change in our theoretical understanding of the processes involved in learning and in the way we view children with learning and behaviour problems. These changes deserve some consideration.

The shift in values is evident not just in the context of education. The civil rights movement in the United States, changes in the status of women and the working class over the past 40 years, and the abolition of apartheid in South Africa all testify to an increased appreciation of the rights of individuals within society. This groundswell shift in cultural values is reflected in the changes observed in many countries in the provision of education for people with disabilities, moving from no special provision at all, through segregated settings towards integration into the mainstream school, and then inclusion (Miron and Katoda 1991). This significant change in values dictates a new discourse, a new way of thinking about special education (McLeskey and Waldron 1996).

The second change has been characterized by some as a broadening of our conception of the individual (Brinker 1990; Schmid 1987), or at least as an extension of our understanding of the variables which should be subjected to analysis in diagnosis, assessment and intervention planning in schools (Barnett *et al.* 1997). Through the 1960s and 1970s, special education practitioners and researchers tacitly assumed that any and all problems of students were located within the students themselves (see, for example, Deno 1970). At that time educational psychologists and others involved in assessment for special education were typically focused on the identification and classification of students in need of special instructional programmes. Such assessments were directed in the main at the academic and social skills and deficits of the individual, in order to discover underlying disabilities or dysfunctions and cognitive strengths and weaknesses which could then be remedied through special educational techniques. Influenced in part by the applied behaviour analysts (Nelson and Polsgrove 1984), ecological psychologists (Barker 1968; Willems 1973) and social learning theorists such as Vygotsky and Bronfenbrenner, the field has moved over time to the point where learning is now usually conceptualized in the literature as an interactive and contextualized process (Will 1988). The environment, both social and physical, is recognized as a powerful determinant of learning and behaviour (Barnett *et al.* 1997; Cullinan *et al.* 1991; Landesman and Ramey 1989). This has resulted in an extension of what we need to consider when we attempt to understand learning and behaviour (Barnett *et al.* 1997). Adequate assessment and intervention is now understood to involve the examination of both the performance of the individual and the quality of the ecological context in which learning is to occur (Ysseldyke and Christenson 1993). As was noted by Schmid (1987), this ecological perspective has changed the focus of interventions in special education 'from treatment to teaching and to learning rather than personality change' (1987: 5).

The two strands described above have, in combination, produced a considerable ethical, philosophical and political move towards educational practices that reflect naturalistic interventions, equity, the placing of students in the least restrictive environment and the inclusion of all students with their peers in regular educational settings. The traditional conceptualization of special education, with its emphasis on classification and individual remediation, does not foster the development of these new kinds of solutions. A new paradigm is emerging, based on an inclusionist ecological perspective of learning and behaviour. This perspective increasingly challenges the traditional assumptions of internal causation and subsequent remediation of identified deficits. This new paradigm postulates that the primary problems facing people with disabilities are external rather than internal (Moore *et al.* 1999). The task of educators working within this paradigm is to alter, adapt and improve educational organizations and environments to meet the needs of all students. Such adaptation of environments is a necessary pre-condition for the successful inclusion of all students in regular education (Udvari-Solnar 1994, 1995).

Paradigm shift to inclusion

Skrtic (1995) argued that adequate understanding of the concept of inclusion involves just such a paradigm shift from individual classification and remediation to creating more inclusive classroom environments. He deliberately labelled this as a shift in paradigm, rather than simply an issue of implementation, because it requires a new way of thinking about the education of students with special needs. Conceptual paradigms determine the arena of inquiry and by their nature constrain one's perspective and determine the kinds of questions asked or solutions sought (Kuhn 1970). At present, there are two paradigms operating in special education or, as Meyen (1995) puts it, special education is currently 'between stories'; namely, between the time-honoured beliefs and assumptions about individual deficit (the functional limitations paradigm) and the emerging inclusive and ecological paradigm (see also Hahn 1989).

Advocates for inclusion (Gartner and Lipsky 1987; Reynolds *et al.* 1987; Stainback and Stainback 1990) argue that the issue is not how to fit students with special needs into regular schools but how to develop schools that fit, nurture and support the educational and social needs of every student. Stainback and Stainback (1990) argue that 'To achieve inclusive schooling general and special educators must come together in a unified, consistent effort' (1990: 3). Thus, this paradigm shift in special education reflects a larger development in general education and indeed in society – a questioning of the basic beliefs that shape education and social practices. The inclusion movement in special education can rightly be subsumed under the umbrella of the multicultural education movement. Multicultural education, also born out of the Civil Rights movement of 1960s and 1970s with an initial focus on countering racism, is now a more generic term for a broad-based school reform movement addressing equity issues related to race, ethnicity, gender, socio-economic class, language and disability (Grant and Tate 1995).

Multicultural education

Issues associated with cultural diversity in education, perhaps more than any other, highlight the potential harm that intervention strategies based on the functional limitations paradigm might have for dealing with individual differences. Students from minority, migrant and refugee cultures frequently encounter learning difficulties arising from the mismatch between the pedagogical assumptions of the classroom and student expectations of how instruction should be delivered (see Humpage 1998). Working in this paradigm, learning and teaching difficulties associated with, for example, differences in oral and written English language competence within the class, may be seen as a deficit, ascribed either to individual students or to the ethnic or cultural group to which they belong. Conversely, an inclusionist and ecological perspective would see this problem as being located within the teacher and the classroom environment she or he creates. As described in Chapter 3, effective language learning contexts build on students' strengths in their first language and expertise in their home culture (Glynn and Glynn 1986; Tavener and Glynn 1989).

Education systems are slowly coming to understand that students' ethnicity and culture exert a major influence over what they do or do not learn at school (Peterson and Ishii-Jordan 1994) and educational policy change and development in light of this changing conceptualization can be an important impetus for change at what Bronfenbrenner (1992) described as the macrosystem level, which may impact directly on the adjustment of refugee children as they settle into school in their new country. It may be instructive, therefore, to look in some detail at recent policy developments in education, and special education in particular, in one country, New Zealand, with a view to considering how such macro developments may impact upon educational provision for refugee children.

The New Zealand context

Special provision for less successful learners in New Zealand was first established with the advent of special classes in 1917 with a rapid expansion of a basically segregated special education system through to the mid-1970s. As with the rest of the Western world this development was characterized by a rather piecemeal approach to policy development generally; in fact there was no formal special education policy in the country until

1996 when the policy statement Special Education 2000 was first published. However, prior to this, a move towards a more inclusive education system was evident, first in the Draft Review of Special Education (1967), then in an official directive supporting the mainstreaming of students with special needs with a non-categorical, needs-based system of support (Department of Education 1988). In 1989, this was mandated with the passage of the New Zealand Education Act, and in 1991 the Ministry of Education recommended the introduction of a needs-based system for resourcing. Special Education 2000 put in place a structure for special education support which guarantees the right for all children to an education in the regular education system, supported on a basis of educational need rather than on psychometric diagnosis (see Brown *et al.* 2000). Importantly, under this policy structure, special education services within New Zealand can provide preventative support for teachers and administrators and can be accessed directly to provide support for the education of refugee children in New Zealand schools.

As has been pointed out previously (Thomson 1998), these changes in special education must be viewed in the context of changes in education in general, which in turn reflect changes in society. There have been major economic, social and demographic changes in New Zealand in recent years; the population has become more culturally and ethnically diverse as waves of migrant groups have been absorbed into the country; and there has also been a growing recognition of the unique position of Maori in New Zealand society, with associated attempts to implement the Treaty of Waitangi more effectively.

In 1990, New Zealand underwent a major educational restructuring designed to separate policy from operations, and schools from central control. The policy documents associated with these changes recognize the diversity of New Zealand society and give clear direction towards a more inclusive system of education. Every school is now a self-governing entity governed by an elected board of trustees. This board enters into a contractual arrangement with the Crown. The National Educational Guidelines (Ministry of Education 1997) form a major part of these contractual arrangements and a basis for audit and review. These guidelines are part of every school charter by law and therefore provide key indicators for the way in which education is to be managed and delivered: indicators which underscore the responsibilities of each school to provide safe and effective inclusive education for all students.

The national educational guidelines

The guidelines have three components: the National Education Goals (NEGS), the National Curriculum Framework, and the National Administration Guidelines (NAGS).

The National Education Goals are broad aims to guide policies and practices. These goals stipulate a legal requirement for boards of trustees to:

- ensure the highest standards of achievement through programmes which enable all students to realize their full potential as individuals and to develop the values needed to become full members of New Zealand's society
- recognize the importance of equal opportunities for all
- give particular consideration to those with special needs
- encourage respect for ethnic diversity within New Zealand.

The New Zealand Curriculum Framework (Ministry of Education 1993), as the official policy for teaching and learning in New Zealand schools, sets out the essential learning areas and essential skills for all students and indicates the important place of attitude and values education in the school curriculum. The New Zealand curriculum applies to 'all students irrespective of gender, ethnicity, belief, ability or disability, social or cultural background or geographical area' (1993: 3).

The National Administration Guidelines specify what boards of trustees must do regarding curriculum and instruction. Of particular relevance to this discussion are the requirements that boards must analyse barriers to learning and achievement, and develop and implement strategies which address identified learning needs in order to overcome barriers to students' learning. The NAGS note that barriers may arise from a number of factors such as student characteristics, home circumstances, school systems and practices, cultural influences and environmental issues. Strategies for overcoming these barriers are identified as possibly occurring at the level of classroom practice, or as involving school-wide changes and the involvement of outside agencies and parent and community groups.

Inclusive education: implications

In addition to the structural or systemic influences of a national inclusive policy on school environments, there are also specific lessons for refugee education which can be derived from current research and practice on the teaching and learning of special populations. The first concerns assessment. There is a consensus emerging among researchers that there is little empirical evidence to show that efforts to plan instructional interventions based on decontextualized assessment of learner characteristics makes a difference to learning and adjustment outcomes (Brinker 1990; Ysseldyke and Christenson 1987). There is mounting evidence that these categorizing processes may disadvantage students, particularly those from culturally and linguistically different homes (Cole 1996). Refugees fit squarely into this situational context. Not only are there concerns that norm-referenced psychometric tests may not be equally valid measures for such groups and therefore likely to lead to unfair outcomes (Ulibarri 1990, cited in Cole, 1996), but the resultant label in itself may contribute to educational disadvantage (Fairbanks 1992; Osborne *et al.* 1991). Once a 'reason' is identified for a child's lack of achievement, there are often no further investigations to seek alternative explanations either within the child (Kube and Shapiro 1996; Sanmiguel *et al.* 1996) or the learning environment (Moore *et al.* 1999). The inclusive/ecological paradigm is based on assumptions about causality which lead to assessing the suitability of the learning environment and support provided for students. Curriculum-based (Mehrens and Clarisio 1993, cited in Cole 1996) and performance or 'portfolio-based' assessment processes attempt to identify obstacles to more effective learning. If an assessment is to provide the basis for effective intervention, it requires an analysis of the student behaviours in the problem context. This is necessary in order to identify family or school variables that may influence performance, current levels of performance for educationally meaningful behaviours, and specification of goals or expectations for performance. Within the refugee education context this will require the clear documentation and understanding of the impact of the migration experience of the refugees.

A second important issue is the acknowledgement that regular classroom teachers need support (Trump 1990; Wilson 1991; York and Tundidor 1995) and training (Gavrilidou *et al.* 1993; Sloper and Tyler 1992; Vaughn *et al.* 1998; Wehby *et al.* 1997), and that programmes and interventions required to facilitate inclusion need to be developed in collaboration with schools at a local level if they are to be utilized and implemented effectively (Gersten *et al.* 1997). These concerns can be addressed by employing professionals skilled at working with schools to develop and implement required changes, and who can work within the system and support regular teachers, thereby ensuring that regular teachers acquire skills and expertise in inclusive assessment and teaching strategies. Refugee children will often require both psychological and linguistic interventions; consequently skilled professionals in these areas need to be drawn into servicing schools with refugee populations.

Conceptually the development of inclusive programmes is no different from any other change in school and teaching practice. As with any educational innovation, the way in which new practices are introduced is important if they are not to be resisted or actively sabotaged (Brown 1992; Fullan 1994; Fullan and Newton 1988). Several specific conditions have been identified as likely to promote teacher acceptance of change. The new practices must be consistent with and close to existing practice and seen to benefit all students in their classes (Gersten *et al.* 1997). Teachers also need support in providing appropriate instruction for students with learning and behaviour problems in ways that are inclusive of the diversity of children in their classes. Schumm and Vaughn (1995) indicate that 'Mentioning strategies is not enough. Teachers must have clear examples of how strategies work for different types of students and how to orchestrate the whole' (Schumm and Vaughn 1995; Sindelar and Kilgore 1995: 352) (see Chapter 6 for a related discussion).

Where failure at school is seen as a problem within the child, psychometric assessment and remedial teaching are central to the work of special educators. However, inclusive instruction requires a different set of skills of the special educator. Support personnel need to be able to assess the environment and the individual in interaction, to collaborate with all other agencies involved, including parents and regular class teachers, to develop programmes, and to facilitate required systems-change within the regular education setting. All these support personnel skills will be critical in facilitating the mutual adaptation of refugees and schools.

The inclusion/ecological paradigm also has implications for school leaders. It is difficult for individual classroom teachers to develop an inclusive classroom if they are not supported by inclusive practices throughout the school. It needs to be acknowledged that principals and teachers need considerable support for the period it takes to develop inclusive school systems. This support can come via specialized funding programmes from government agencies as well as from the development of national policies in refugee education and language.

Moore *et al.* (1999), on reviewing the special education literature, noted the seemingly marginal role generally assigned to parents, families and the community in the provision of special education for children with learning and behaviour problems. By contrast an inclusive/ecological perspective, by its very nature, requires parental involvement in every aspect of the educational process (see, for example, Eber 1996). The need for maximum coordination across settings (school, home and community), involving teachers and parents in the planning and provision of services, has now been clearly recognized (Wilson 1991). For interventions to address problem behaviours successfully, the behaviours need to be addressed in all settings in which they occur (Day *et al.* 1994). Schools cannot successfully work alone. The education of refugees requires the integration of multiple initiatives aimed at increasing the child's access to schools and parental involvement in schools. One way to increase the effectiveness of educational provision and to involve parents and the community more directly (Eber 1996; Ruma *et al.* 1996; Wassef *et al.* 1996) is to involve them as full partners in the decision-making process concerning the education of their children (Gorney and Ysseldyke 1993; Lange and Ysseldyke 1998). To this end, it is important for schools to develop consensus-building strategies to facilitate the development of working partnerships between parents, teachers and all other stakeholders (Lange and Ysseldyke 1994).

Several attempts to develop coordination between parents and educators (Wang *et al.* 1991) have been identified. Sanders and Epstein (1998) have demonstrated that partnerships with parents can be particularly advantageous to students, especially those from economically disadvantaged families and from ethnic minorities. On arrival in their new country, refugees may find themselves in both categories, often for the first time. The children's school may well be the most convenient and accessible institution to which refugee parents can turn but for this to work well schools need to develop positive, comprehensive partnerships with the families. This involves breaking down barriers to effective communication (for example, a lack of language skills), and helping families to overcome their reluctance to use the school as a resource. Harris (1996), in discussing the processes of collaboration within a multicultural society, emphasizes that developing cultural competence is important for professionals working in inclusive education. Developing effective learning and teaching strategies for students of minority cultural groups requires consultants and teachers to learn to think, explain and act according to predominant metaphors and theories of these cultures, and not simply in terms of the metaphors and theories of their own (majority) culture.

An essential feature of inclusive education is that accountability for the education of all students rests with personnel in each school. Acceptance of this responsibility within schools will require adequate resourcing to address two strategies: providing for the needs of individual students and providing for changing the knowledge and understanding of teachers, parents and communities. This parallels the arguments for establishing effective multicultural education practices through both empowering the minority and enlightening the majority (Banks 1988). Specifically, it will require pre-service teacher education to focus on inclusive teaching strategies; continuing class-wide and school-wide support for teachers in adapting curriculum and teaching strategies, including increased teacher awareness of different cultures and their experiences; and continuing professional development support for existing teachers, boards and principals.

One final noteworthy policy challenge is the challenge to keep the intent of the policy intact in its implementation. Policy is rarely implemented as intended (Timperley and Robinson 1997); consequently, policy development and implementation is likely to be compromised and become contradictory. Paradigm shifts require a fundamental change in thinking (Skrtic 1995) and an implication from this for policy makers is the need to provide an ongoing programme of professional development that supports schools and regular class teachers in becoming skilled in educational practices that will support the effective instruction of all. Such skills alone are likely to be insufficient, however, and teachers must also have the opportunity to develop a sound understanding of the principles and values of inclusive education and additional tools and methods to enable them to better cater for the needs of a more diverse group of students.

Chapter 8

Education of refugee children
Documenting and implementing change

Richard Hamilton and Dennis Moore

As indicated in Chapter 1, our goal in developing a model for the education of refugee children is to facilitate understanding of the wide range of factors which may have an impact on their adjustment to school and to outline approaches to assessment and intervention for this diverse group. The theoretical and empirical material reviewed in previous chapters contributes to this model by underscoring the significant role played by families, schools and other helping services in the adaptation of refugee children to their new host country as well as to their educational progress. The developmental model can help us conceptualize the array of individual and environmental factors that may hinder or facilitate the process of adaptation (the task faced by refugees). In addition, we can employ the model to track and describe change over time. Significant intra- and interpersonal and systemic diagnostic indicators have been identified which can signal successful and less successful adaptation and integration. Thus the model enables the critical examination of programmes and structures which may be put in place to support the processes of adaptation and integration.

The separation of the refugee child's development into *migratory phases* (pre-, trans- and post-phases) and the adoption of an *ecological perspective* (micro-, meso-, exo- and macrosystems) (see Figure 1.1) are key features of the model developed in the collected papers in this volume. It is clear that experiences which occur within each of the migratory phases can impact refugee children's development and adaptation within the host society schools. Stressors that occur within the different phases cannot be considered in isolation. Refugee children carry their past experiences with them, including their understanding of their roles and expectations within their former social ecosystems and the disjunctures that have either caused or been caused by the process of forced migration. They have to adjust to new demands caused by marked and frequently concurrent changes to their social ecosystem which occur as they move from pre-migration to trans-migration and post-migration contexts. Refugees often move to countries that are quite different from their own. The major task for the refugee child and family is to manage this transition as smoothly as possible, and to adjust to the existing social ecosystems as well as develop mutually satisfying ecosystems.

The particular focus of this book is on the host countries' educational systems and ways in which these might be adapted in order to support this transition process and optimize the effective inclusion of refugee children in their new schools. In coming to some understanding of what an effective and adapting education system might look like, we have relied heavily on Bronfenbrenner's theorizing regarding the ecological nature of human development. This perspective contrasts with others that could have been employed (for example, medical, psychiatric, psychological, sociological) and provides a useful and integrative conceptual frame in which to consider theory and research originating from these other perspectives. A review of this work has allowed the identification of what we believe are key indicators of both the resilience of the refugee child and his or her personal micro- and mesosystems, and the supportive qualities of the school system in which the refugee child is placed. Our intent in reviewing a broad array of research literature from a variety of disciplinary perspectives was to create a model which would apply across different refugee populations and host country education systems.

In the preceding chapters we have identified a variety of contributing factors within each of the phases of refugee migration, while also considering the interacting effects of factors working at different levels of the social ecosystem. These factors can be used in the development and evaluation of educational interventions for refugee children (see Table 8.1). As can be seen in Table 8.1, these diagnostic indicators include specific characteristics of the refugee children and their parents including the degree of pre-migration trauma, the mental health status of the child and parents, the degree of family cohesion, literacy proficiency in first and second languages and prior educational experience of the student. All of these may represent ongoing risk factors which can interfere with adaptation to school. Unresolved emotional issues associated with displacement and trauma in the past can clearly interfere with the child's ability to learn and develop within school. Similarly, the ease with which a child's family manages to adapt to its new circumstances will influence the extent to which the child can adapt to the social and educational requirements of the new school. Importantly, however, a range of characteristics of schools' organization and instruction, and indeed the broader educational and social policy of the host country, are also at play in the process of adaptation. In addition, support services available in the host country, and the degree to which these are coordinated to help children and families, can either facilitate or present a barrier to this process of adaptation. All of these factors which exist at different systemic levels within the child's ecosystem can influence the effectiveness of any intervention aimed at the education of the refugee child.

It is important to emphasize that adaptation is a mutual process. Schools, teachers and class peers most likely to have positive effects on

Table 8.1 Diagnostic indicators of adaptation and development for refugee education

---

Pre-/Trans-migration factors

Personal

- extent of trauma
- mental health status
- literacy – first and second language proficiency
- coping styles/resilience
- previous educational experience

Familial

- degree of familial separation/extent of loss and bereavement
- degree of family cohesion

Post-migration factors

Both personal and familial pre- and trans-migration factors can continue to either interfere with or facilitate adaptation to school. In addition, an array of personal, familial and school/community-based factors can also impact adaptation post-migration.

Personal

- extent of loss and bereavement
- second language proficiency
- personal resilience
- attitudes toward both own and host societies

Familial

- parental depression
- family functioning
- degree of family and community cohesion
- strength of home culture presence in host country
- degree of difference/distance between family values and values of typical host families
- socio-demographic variables (residence and employment status, ages, religion, and so on)
- immigration status and family unification

School and community-based factors

- teacher skills, awareness and receptivity
- host country student attitudes
- teacher experience and attitudes
- school structure and policies
- targeted induction processes
- first and second language support
- availability of community services
- level of communication between schools and families
- positive and supportive school environment
- governmental policies and initiatives
- coordinated support plans which integrate child, family, school and community
- coordinated interagency support

Outcomes

In considering the success of any refugee educational intervention, attention should be focused not only on the individual child's adaptation as evidenced by changes in child behaviour, learning, peer relations and health, but also the school's adaptation as evidenced by changes in school policies, procedures, practices and teacher development.

- increased levels of self-esteem
- appropriate academic progress
- increased second language proficiency
- children's and parents' psychological adjustment
- parental support and involvement in child's education
- increased communication between family and schools
- positive changes in teacher attitudes, knowledge and skills
- positive attitudes toward the new immigrants within the host society
- effective systems for recognizing, monitoring and referring students experiencing difficulties

refugee children are characterized by a willingness to make changes for the benefit of refugee children.

A defining feature of Bronfenbrenner's (1992) ecological theory is the interdependence of the different ecosystems. Even positive change at one point can have an adverse effect on other parts of the ecosystem, and it is important to monitor for such unintended effects. To illustrate, host country language development is clearly a need for many refugee children. In response to this need, schools might be expected to develop a capacity for intensive support for second language acquisition for their students. However, improved language facility on the part of the refugee students increases their capacity to make their anxieties and frustrations known to teachers and peers, thereby increasing the possibility of new conflicts and tensions. Schools need to examine current mechanisms for fostering positive communication and resolving such conflict within their community. New stresses within a refugee family may occur as another, often unanticipated, impact of a successful second-language programme within a school. Parents may find themselves in a role reversal situation within their families, relying on their children in new and unaccustomed ways simply because of their children's greater facility in the host country language. This in turn may have a detrimental impact on the adult's personal and social identity, particularly as these are often already challenged by experiences of relative poverty and underemployment. To address this aspect of the child's social microsystem may involve the school in negotiating (or providing) community-based language teaching in order to help both the refugee child and family to adapt more comfortably.

Working within an ecologically focused developmental model, we have identified throughout the preceding chapters in this volume a number of factors which can impact for good or ill on the adjustment of refugee students to their new schools. In planning for the provision of educational support for refugee students, attention should be paid to pre- and trans-migratory factors which may influence adjustment and it is important that initial assessments of student needs take these into account. However, in planning, it is also important to assess the status of educational provision in the post-migration 'here-and-now', as it is here in particular that we are able to move from a reactive remedial position to more proactively adapting our educational provision to better cater for these students' current needs. In the following sections, we will focus on what we can do in the post-migration phase to create a high quality educational environment for refugee children.

The education of refugee children: best practice

As indicated in Chapter 1, one of the major tasks facing the refugee child when arriving in a new country is to adapt to a new school environment. It is important to note that in order for the refugee child to adapt effectively, schools, teachers and student peers will also need to adapt. Our purpose in this chapter is to consider how best to prepare to meet the needs of these refugee children.

Although there is still a need for research concerning how best to help refugee children progress within schools, there is much that we can say about how to adapt our educational provision to better cater for these children's needs. Within the previous chapters, we organized our discussion around areas of research which contribute to our understanding of refugees and their education. The focus of the following discussion will be on what schools (principals and teachers) and those who govern schools (boards and government education agencies) can do to create the best possible educational environment for refugee children. The discussion will be organized to address: national educational policy; school structure and policy; school–family–community interface; classroom environment and instruction; and teacher professional development.

National educational policy and initiatives

As suggested in Chapter 7, the success of educational interventions within schools will require clear government policies on the support and education of refugee children. This aspect of the macrosystem may determine the direction and viability of local level initiatives intended to enhance the education of the refugee child.

In order to ensure the possibility of success of school interventions, countries need to consider the development of a comprehensive national policy on refugee education. Such a policy should address governance, coordination and the financial support of services for newly arrived refugees. In addition, given the potentially far-reaching negative social and fiscal effects of unsuccessful acculturation by newly arrived non-voluntary migrant groups, the national policy needs also to address issues of multicultural adaptation in our increasingly pluralist societies. Negative outcomes of unsuccessful acculturation are largely avoidable, but to avoid them involves significant change of attitude at the policy level and by the population as a whole, as well as at the level of the local school. A national policy will need to support and address two strategies for teaching refugees – providing for the needs of individual students and providing for changing the knowledge and understanding of teachers, parents and communities.

Language issues should occupy a central role in the development and content of a national policy on the education of refugee children. The usual staffing levels for ESOL students will need strengthening to ensure adequate support when working with refugee students who frequently bring emotional as well as language needs to the school. In addition, the need to engage bicultural workers fluent in the native language of the refugees puts an extra burden on the existing school resources. Further, as is true with most migration situations, schools will require additional instructional and assessment materials within the native language of the refugee target groups (for example, bilingual dictionaries, reading material in the refugee's first language, and instruction booklets focused on language difficulties of specific refugee populations).

The national policy should also address ways to facilitate the collaboration of services across multiple service providers. Refugees require a wide range of coordinated support on arrival (for example, health care, help with finding accommodation and employment, access to counselling services and interpreters, and language training). Consequently, energy needs to be directed toward the development of networking, integration and collaboration between these services.

In order to optimize the productive use of additional resources directed at the support of refugees, these resources should be allocated in ways that facilitate speedy and flexible use at the local level (see Hamilton *et al.* 2001). The centralized targeting of funds for specific needs may limit the schools' ability to employ the funds to best serve the needs of the refugee students. In addition, government support to non-government refugee service providers needs to be flexible enough to allow a degree of latitude in the employment of the funds to cater for sometimes unexpected needs. This will support local refugee service teams in creating the best possible environment to assist in the integration and education of refugee families and children.

If there is not a well-thought out national policy on the provision of services for the education of refugees, local activities intended to support them are likely to be reactive, piecemeal and uncoordinated. Such an approach to the education of refugee children is unlikely to be very successful. However, it is important that programmes and interventions derived from such a policy aimed at facilitating educational inclusion for refugee children are developed in collaboration with schools at a local level.

In addition to the above suggestions related to the development of a national policy on the education of refugee children, Table 8.2 identifies other domains, such as the development of curriculum, training of teachers and the employment of professionals to help schools in the education of refugee children, which are unlikely to be addressed without national policy leadership.

School structure and policy

A prevailing theme throughout this book (see Chapters 2, 4, 5 and 6) is the importance of creating a safe educational environment for refugee children. The grief, loss and trauma literature emphasizes the importance of creating therapeutic means for refugee children to cope with their experience. The literature on resilience offers a dynamic perspective, focusing on positive

Table 8.2 Best practice suggestions: national educational policy and initiatives

- pre-service teacher education needs to focus on inclusive teaching strategies, methods of increasing teacher awareness of different cultures and their experiences, and the plight and experiences of refugees
- consultants and teachers must learn to think, explain and act according to the predominant metaphors and theories of these cultures, in order to develop effective learning and teaching strategies for refugee students
- schools and education authorities must employ professionals skilled at working with schools to develop and implement required changes
- policy makers need to provide an ongoing programme of professional development that supports schools and regular class teachers throughout the country to become skilled in inclusive educational practices which focus on refugees
- educators of refugee children need to develop consensus building strategies to facilitate the development of working partnerships between parents, teachers and all other stakeholders
- schools and policy makers must work together to develop a curriculum that includes human rights and cultural diversity dimensions

outcomes. School-based interventions can be structured to promote the development of resilience. Education systems are coming to understand that students' ethnicity and culture exert a major influence over what they learn at school. Attention needs to be devoted to validating the refugee child's culture and experience while also providing understanding of cultural expectations within the host country. Programmes which cater for culturally diverse instructional needs and encourage the appreciation of cultural diversity are particularly useful in the prevention of learning difficulties and behaviour problems for these students. Table 8.3 includes a list of suggestions regarding school structures and policies that are intended to ensure that they can learn and grow within a safe and supportive environment.

School–family–community interface

As indicated in Chapter 6, effective schools typically include efficient mechanisms for involving parents and the surrounding community in the education of their children. Within the context of educating refugee children, this involvement is particularly important as in this way the school can also directly affect the quality of life of the parents and the surrounding community (for example, through language classes and adult education classes) and also benefit from the skills and expertise of parents and individuals within the relevant cultural community. Schools can employ social events and gatherings as a vehicle for creating lines of communication with parents and for helping parents to network among themselves and others within the community. Employing members of the target refugee community within schools (as bilingual teacher aide or

Table 8.3 Best practice suggestions: school structures and policy

- ensure induction processes are explicit and clearly developed
- develop and apply policies for eliminating racism and bullying
- implement or strengthen cross-cultural curricular topics and projects within schools, to help increase levels of understanding, acceptance and mutual respect
- appoint a caring adult or mentor (teachers or counsellors) to look out for children in need
- include structured opportunity for social interaction (e.g. peer support programmes), thereby creating a nurturing, accepting and caring school climate.
- implement programmes that promote the development of student self-esteem, internal locus of control, and good social skills
- enable students from the host country to participate in programmes to expand their knowledge of different cultures, importance of diversity in the classroom, human rights and the plight of refugees

tutors) and in refugee helping services also builds trust between and within these groups.

An inclusive/ecological perspective requires the involvement of parents as full partners in every aspect of the educational planning, decision-making process, and provision of services for their refugee children. The more that members of the surrounding community and parents are involved in the education of their refugee children, the more likely it will be that their children will thrive within schools. Table 8.4 includes some additional best practice ideas for facilitating communication between the different stakeholders as well as their involvement in schools.

Classroom environment and instruction

The immediate educational environment of the refugee child should focus on helping the child acquire meta-knowledge that will support their learning and development. Of particular importance for most refugees will be the development of appropriate language skills. Also, as refugee children's educational experiences may have been very different from typical educational experiences within the host country, there may be a contrast in expectations regarding classroom norms between the teacher and school on the one hand, and those of the refugee child on the other. It is important to focus on creating collegial environments, so children can learn from and about each other. As noted in Chapter 3, cooperative learning and peer tutoring strategies may be particularly useful in this process (Brown and Thomson 2000).

Many of the suggestions for best practice presented in Table 8.5 focus on language issues, given the importance of language development in allowing the refugee child to successfully participate in schools and classrooms.

Table 8.4 Best practice suggestions: school–family–community interface

- increase positive and culturally appropriate liaison between schools and families, which includes programmes for parents participating in school enterprises, or school forums to foster cultural diversity and communication
- ensure schools are provided with clear avenues for seeking and acquiring specialist support and assistance when faced with children who are traumatized
- ensure the purposes of relevant refugee helping services and the identity of contact individuals within these organizations are known to school staff for when they have specific questions and needs related to the education of refugee children
- ensure school-based, family and social and individual therapeutic interventions are interlinked to reconstruct a sense of social belonging
- teach the host language to both children and adults to facilitate the development of social networks
- make local information available to refugee families to alleviate some of the stress associated with relocation
- involve all parties in the design and delivery of programmes and services
- develop effective communication channels between the school and home
- ensure educators of refugee children develop consensus building strategies to help establish working partnerships between parents, teachers and other stakeholders

Teachers will need to acquire increased knowledge and skills related to multicuturalism, cultural responsiveness, traumatized children, and inclusive approaches to assessment and education (see the section below on professional development for teachers). This increased knowledge and skill will clearly impact on the nature of classroom environments and instruction.

Table 8.5 Best practice suggestions: classroom environment and instruction

- assess both first (L1) and second (L2) language at entry and at regular intervals in order to develop appropriate educational experiences for the refugee child
- include refugee children who need to learn the language of the host country in mainstream classes to increase their exposure to English speaking peers and to decrease stigmatization
- develop withdrawal ESOL classes to meet specific needs of refugee students
- link the curriculum content of withdrawal ESOL classes to content courses to maximize relevancy
- develop a peer tutoring or a buddy system to provide learners with knowledgeable host country peers
- create opportunities for refugee students to raise issues important to them in order to help them feel that their first language and culture are respected
- use group processes in class to facilitate the development of friendships for refugees
- encourage and foster the maintenance of the language of origin

Principal leadership and teacher professional development

The literature on effective schools reviewed in Chapter 6 underscores the importance of proactive leadership and active support for innovation by teachers. This is particularly important when schools are adopting alternative approaches to teaching or implementing a new curriculum (such as a programme for teaching refugee students).

Within the context of refugee education, the principal can play a vital role in leading and supporting teacher development and in the use of new techniques which are useful in helping refugee students adapt to a new school environment. Table 8.6 lists some suggestions to facilitate teacher implementation of new skills and techniques. Principals should play a leadership role in supporting teachers in adapting their classrooms and lessons to the needs of refugee children (see Table 8.6).

Finally, the principal also acts as a gatekeeper and facilitator in the use of community and agency helping services and the integration of school support systems into this network.

Professional development of teachers

As discussed in Chapter 6, teacher expectations can significantly influence the type of environment that they create for individual students within the classroom. Given that refugees often come from very different cultures and possess different values and goals from those held by members of the country within which they are settling, the potential for conflict in teacher–student interactions is heightened. Consequently, initiatives aimed at influencing teacher views, knowledge and expectations related to the culture of the incoming refugee students need to be part of any attempt to have a significant impact on refugee education.

Table 8.6 Best practice suggestions: principal leadership

- emphasize the benefits of gaining new skills and knowledge for teaching refugee students
- include teachers in decisions about how best to teach refugee children within their classrooms
- help teachers tailor new skills and knowledge to their specific classroom, their teaching styles and content
- create a mechanism which allows teachers to express their concerns and have those concerns answered
- create small group or departmental supportive settings for teachers to discuss sensitive issues or any anxieties they may have when working with refugee youths
- publicly support the initiatives within the school and in the community for facilitating the education of refugee children

In Table 8.7, we have identified a number of knowledge domains relevant to the professional practice of teachers working with refugees as students. Clearly, ensuring this knowledge base is available to teachers requires a significant commitment to refugee education not only from the principal of the school but also from relevant boards of trustees, communities and government agencies and officials.

In conclusion, considerable research effort has gone into addressing the challenge of creating vital educational environments for refugee children and others at the margins of our education system. One of the challenges we face, however, is that what has been learned from research is not easily conveyed to practising teachers (Hargreaves 1996). In order for a concerted effort to be made to introduce a cohesive, research-based change to the teaching and learning process, schools must be encouraged and supported in their efforts to educate all our children. This can only be done if there is a common goal and a well-organized and managed support system.

Darling-Hammond (1993: 759) argues that effective change within education systems to address challenges such as those represented by the arrival of refugee families requires three national investments. Firstly, effective educational adaptations of this nature require an alignment of political intention, policy and professional development. Secondly, there must also be a clear policy mandate for the establishment of an environment that supports the intended practice and, finally, there should be an investment in individual and organizational learning.

Table 8.7 Best practice suggestions: professional development of teachers

Professional development should focus on assisting teachers to:

- increase their skills for teaching traumatized children, their knowledge of symptoms and triggers of emotional relapses and their confidence in referring students to appropriate services (when available)
- increase their knowledge of the nature of forced migration and its influence on refugee children—for example, helping teachers become familiar with the different pre-, trans- and post-migration factors which influence the development of refugee children should be a focus on professional development (see Table 8.1)
- increase their knowledge of issues related to diversity
- increase their knowledge of the different refugee cultures and communities
- acquire skills to employ curriculum-based and performance or 'portfolio-based' assessment processes focused on identifying obstacles to more effective learning
- acquire 'culturally responsive' approaches to teaching all children; i.e. skills and expertise in inclusive assessment and teaching strategies
- acquire skills for helping refugee children with the task of second language learning and acculturation (i.e. this is the responsibility of all teachers not just ESOL teachers)
- learn to think, explain and act according to predominant metaphors and theories of relevant refugee cultures

Bibliography

Ahearn, F. L., Jr. and Athey, J. L. (1991) 'The mental health of refugee children: an overview', in F. L. Ahearn Jr. and J. L. Athey (eds) *Refugee Children: Theory, Research, and Services* (pp. 3–19), Washington, DC: MCH Bureau.

Almqvist, K. and Brandell-Forsberg, M. (1995) 'Iranian refugee children in Sweden: effects of organized violence and forced migration on preschool children', *American Journal of Orthopsychiatry*, 65: 225–37.

Almqvist, K. and Brandell-Forsberg, M. (1997) 'Refugee children in Sweden: post-traumatic stress disorder in Iranian preschool children exposed to organized violence', *Child Abuse and Neglect*, 21: 351–66.

Almqvist, K. and Broberg, A. G. (1997) 'Silence and survival: working with strategies of denial in families of traumatized pre-school children', *Journal of Child Psychotherapy*, 23: 417–35.

American Psychiatric Association (1994) *American Psychiatric Association Diagnostic and Statistical Manual of Mental Disorders* (4th edn), Washington.

Banks, J. A. (1988) *Multiethnic Education: Theory and Practice* (2nd edn), Boston, MA: Allyn and Bacon.

Banks, J. (1993) 'Multicultural education: Development, dimensions and challenges', *Phi Delta Kappan*, 75, 22–28.

Barker, R. G. (1968) *Ecological Psychology*, Palo Alto, CA: Stanford University Press.

Barnard, R. (1998) 'NESB students: the need for systematic induction to the learning culture of our schools', *Many Voices*, 13: 4–7.

Barnett, D. W., Lentz, F. E., Bauer, A. M. and Macmann, G. (1997) 'Ecological foundations of early intervention: planned activities and strategic sampling', *Journal of Special Education*, 30: 471–90.

Barth, R. (1990) *Improving Schools from Within*, San Francisco: Jossey-Bass.

Becker, H. (2001) *Teaching ESL K-12: Views from the Classroom*, Boston, MA: Heinle and Heinle.

Becker, R. (1984) *Parent Involvement: A Review of Research and Principles of Successful Practice*, Washington, DC: National Institute of Education.

Beiser, M., Dion, R., Gotowiec, A., Hyman, I. *et al.* (1995) 'Immigrant and refugee children in Canada', *Canadian Journal of Psychiatry*, 40: 67–72.

Bemak, F. and Greenberg, B. (1994) 'Southeast Asian refugee adolescents: implications for counseling', *Journal of Multicultural Counseling and Development*, 22: 115–24.

Berman, P. and McLaughlin, M. (1980) 'Factors affecting the process of change', in M. Milstein (ed.) *Schools, Conflict and Change*, New York: Teachers College Press.

Berry, J. W. (1987) 'Acculturation and psychological adaptation: a conceptual overview', in J. W. Berry and R. C. Annis (eds) *Ethnic Psychology: Research and Practice with Immigrants, Refugees, Native Peoples, Ethnic Groups and Sojourners* (pp. 41–52), Amsterdam: Swets and Zeitlinger.

Berry, J. W. (1995) 'Psychology of acculturation', in N. R. Goldberger and J. B. Veroff (eds) *The Culture and Psychology Reader* (pp. 457–88), New York: New York University Press.

Berry, J. W. (1999) 'Intercultural relations in plural societies', *Canadian Psychology*, 40: 12–21.

Berry, J. W. (2000) 'Cross-cultural psychology: a symbiosis of cultural and comparative approaches', *Asian Journal of Social Psychology*, 3: 197–205.

Berry, J. W. (2001) 'A psychology of immigration', *Journal of Social Issues*, 57: 615–31.

Bishop, R. and Glynn, T. (1998) 'Achieving cultural integrity in education in Aotearoa/New Zealand', in K. Cushner (ed.) *International Perspectives on Intercultural Education* (pp. 38–69), Mahweh, NJ: Lawrence Erlbaum Associates.

Blechman, E. (2000) 'Resilience', in A. E. Kazdin (ed.) *Encyclopedia of Psychology* Vol. 7, Washington, DC: American Psychological Association.

Bolloten, B. and Spafford, T. (1998) 'Supporting refugee children in East London primary schools', in C. Jones and J. Rutter (eds) *Refugee Education: Mapping the Field* (pp. 107–24), Staffordshire: Trentham Books.

Boua, C. (1990) 'Children of the killing fields: Cambodian adolescents in New South Wales', *Occasional Paper No. 19, Migration & Multicultural Studies*, Wollongong, NSW, Australia: University of Wollongong.

Bourhis, R. Y., Moiese, L. C., Perreault, S. and Senecal, S. (1997) 'Towards an interactive acculturation model: a social psychological approach', *International Journal of Psychology*, 32: 369–86.

Bowlby, J. (1973) *Separation: Anxiety and Anger,* Vol. 2 of *Attachment and Loss*, London: The Hogarth Press.

Bowlby, J. (1980) *Loss: Sadness and Depression*, Vol. 3 of *Attachment and Loss*, New York: Basic Books.

Brinker, R. P. (1990) 'In search of the foundation of special education: who are the individuals and what are the differences? Special Section: The importance of individual differences to special education effectiveness', *Journal of Special Education*, 24: 174–84.

Brizuela, B. and Garcia-Sellers, M. (1999) 'School adaptation: a triangulation process', *American Educational Research Journal*, 36: 183–99.

Bronfenbrenner, U. (1979) *The Ecology of Human Development. Experiments by Nature and Design*, Cambridge, MA: Harvard University Press.

Bronfenbrenner, U. (1992) 'Ecological systems theory', in R. Vasta (ed.) *Six Theories of Child Development: Revised Formulations and Current Issues* (pp. 187–249), London: Jessica Kingsley Publishers.

Bronfenbrenner, U. (1993) 'The ecology of cognitive development: research models and fugitive findings', in R. Wozniak and K. Fischer (eds) *Development in Context*, Hillsdale, NJ: Lawrence Erlbaum Associates.

Bronfenbrenner, U. (1999) 'Environments in developmental perspective: theoretical and operational models', in S. Friedman and T. Wachs (eds) *Measuring*

Environment Across the Life Span: Emerging Methods and Concepts, (pp. 3–28), Washington, DC: American Psychological Association.

Bronfenbrenner, U. and Morris, P. (1999) 'The ecology of the developmental process', in W. Damon and R. Lerner (eds) *Handbook of Child Psychology (5th edn)*, New York: John Wiley and Sons.

Brooks-Gunn, J. (2001) 'Children in families in communities: risk and intervention in the Bronfenbrenner tradition', in P. Moen, G. H. J. Elder, K. Luscher (eds) *Examining Lives in Context: Perspectives on the Ecology of Human Development*, (pp. 467–519), Washington, DC: American Psychological Association.

Brophy, G. (1985) 'Teacher-student interaction', in J. Dusek (ed.) *Teacher Expectancies*, Hillsdale, NJ: Lawrence Erlbaum Associates.

Brown, D. F. (1992) *The Development of Strategic Classrooms in Two Secondary Schools*, Waikanae, New Zealand: Wordsmiths.

Brown, D., Moore, D. W., Thomson, C., Anderson, A., Walker, J., Glynn, T., Macfarlane. A., Medcalf, J. and Ysseldyke, J. (2000) 'Resource teachers learning and behaviour: an ecological approach to special education', *Australasian Journal of Special Education*, 24: 15–20.

Brown, D. and Thomson, C. (2000) *Cooperative Learning in New Zealand Schools*, Palmerston North: Dunmore Press.

Burnett, L. (1998) *Issues in Immigrant Settlement in Australia*, National Centre for English Language Teaching and Research, Macquarie University, Sydney, Australia.

Caplan, N. S., Choy, M. H. and Whitmore, J. K. (1991) *Children of the Boat People: A Story of Educational Success*, Ann Arbor, MI: University of Michigan Press.

Chambon, A. (1989) 'Refugees families' experiences: three family themes - family disruption, violent trauma and acculturation', *Journal of Strategic and Systemic Therapies*, 8: 3–13.

Chubb, J. and Moe, T. (1990) *Politics, Markets, and America's School*, Washington, DC: Brookings Institute.

Chung, R. C.-Y., Bemak, F. and Wong, S. (2000) 'Vietnamese refugees' levels of distress, social support and acculturation: implications for mental health counseling', *Journal of Mental Health Counseling*, 22: 150–61.

Cicchetti, D. and Rogosch, F. A. (1997) 'The role of self-organization in the promotion of resilience in maltreated children', *Development and Psychopathology*, 9: 797–815.

Clark, P. and Millikan, J. (1986) *Developing Multi-cultural Perspectives*, Richmond, Australia: Richmond Multicultural Resource Centre.

Coelho, E. (1994) 'Social integration of immigrant and refugee children', in F. Genesee (ed.) *Educating Second Language Children: The Whole Child, the Whole Curriculum, the Whole Community* (pp. 301–28), Cambridge: Cambridge University Press.

Cole, E. (1996) 'Immigrant and refugee children and families: supporting a new road travelled', in M. G. Luther, E. Cole *et al.* (eds) *Dynamic Assessment for Instruction: From Theory to Application.* (pp. 35–42), North York, ON, Canada: Captus Press.

Collier, V. P. (1987) 'Age and rate of acquisition of second language for academic purposes', *TESOL Quarterly*, 21: 617–41.

Collier, V. P. (1989) 'How Long? A synthesis of research on academic achievement in a second language', *TESOL Quarterly*, 23: 509–31.

Corr, C. and Corr, D. (eds) (1996) *Handbook of Childhood Death and Bereavement*, New York: Springer Publishing Company.

Cortés, C. (1994) 'Multiculturation: an educational model for a culturally and linguistically diverse society', in K. Spangenberg-Urbschat and R. Pritchard (eds), *Kids Come in all Languages: Reading Instruction for ESL Students* (pp. 22–35), Newark, Delaware: International Reading Association.

Creamer, M. (2000) 'Post-traumatic stress disorder following violence and aggression', *Aggression and Violent Behaviour* 5: 431–49.

Creemers, B. and Scheerens, S. (1989) 'Developments in school effectiveness research', *International Journal of Educational Research*, 13: 685–825.

Cullinan, D., Epstein, M. H. and Lloyd, J. W. (1991) 'Evaluation of conceptual models of behavioral disorders', *Behavioral Disorders*, 16: 148-57.

Cummins, J. (1981) *Bilingualism and Minority Children*, Ontario: Ontario Institute for Studies in Education.

Cummins, J. (1988) 'Second language acquisition within bilingual education programs', in L. Beebe (ed.). *Issues in Second Language Acquisition: Multiple Perspectives*, New York: Newbury House Publishers.

Cummins, J. (1994) 'The acquisition of English as a second language', in K. Spangenberg-Urbschat and R. Pritchard (eds) *Kids Come in all Languages: Reading Instruction for ESL Students* (pp. 36–62), Newark, DE: International Reading Association.

Cummins, J. and Swain, M. (1986) *Bilingualism in Education*, New York: Longman.

Cushner, K. (1998a) 'Intercultural education from an international perspective: an introduction', in K. Cushner (ed.) *International Perspectives on Intercultural Education* (pp. 1–13), Mahwah, NJ: Lawrence Erlbaum Associates.

Cushner, K. (1998b) 'Intercultural education from an international perspective: commonalities and future prospects', in K. Cushner (ed.) *International Perspectives on Intercultural Education* (pp. 353–377), Mahwah, NJ: Lawrence Erlbaum Associates.

Darling-Hammond, L. (1993) 'Reframing the school reform agenda: developing capacity for school transformation', *Phi Delta Kappan*, 74: 753–61.

Davison, C. (2001) 'Current policies, programs and practices in school ESL', in B. Mohan, C. Leung and C. Davison (eds) *English as a Second Language in the Mainstream: Teaching, Learning and Identity* (pp. 30–50), Harlow, England: Longman.

Day, H. M., Horner, R. H. and O'Neill, R. E. (1994) 'Multiple functions or problem behaviors: assessment and intervention. Special Issue: Functional analysis approaches to behavioral assessment and treatment', *Journal of Applied Behavior Analysis*, 27: 279–89.

Del Medico, V., Weller, E. and Weller, R. (1996) 'Childhood depression', in L. T. Hechtman *et al.* (eds) *Do They Grow Out Of It? Long-term Outcomes of Childhood Disorders*. (Vol. xv, pp. 101–19), Washington, DC: American Psychiatric Press.

Deno, E. (1970) 'Special education as developmental capital', *Exceptional Children*, 37: 229–37.

Department of Education (1967) *The Draft Review of Education*, Wellington: Department of Education.

Department of Education (1988) *Draft Review of Special Education*, Wellington: Department of Education.

Department of Education and Science (1980) *Report by HM Inspectors on Educational Provision by the Inner London Educational Authority*, London: DES.

Dufresne, J. (1992) 'Mainstreaming Hmong students: for whom and how much?' (ERIC Document Reproduction Service No. ED360700).

Dusek, J. E. (1985) *Teacher Expectancies*, Hillsdale, NJ: Lawrence Erlbaum Associates.

Eber, L. (1996) 'Restructuring schools through the wraparound approach: the LADSE experience', *Special Services in the Schools*, 11: 135–49.

Ehlers, A., Boos, A. and Maercker, A. (2000) 'Posttraumatic stress disorder following political imprisonment: the role of mental defeat, alienation and perceived permanent change', *Journal of Abnormal Psychology*, 109: 45–55.

Eisenbruch, M. (1991) 'From posttraumatic stress disorder to cultural bereavement: diagnosis of Southeast Asian refugees', *Social Science and Medicine*, 33: 673–80.

Ekblad, S. (1993) 'Psychosocial adaptation of children while housed in a Swedish refugee camp: aftermath of the collapse of Yugoslavia', *Stress Medicine*, 9: 159–66.

Ellis, R. (1994) *The Study of Second Language Acquisition*, Oxford: Oxford University Press.

Ellis, R., Loewen, S. and Basturkmen, H. (1999) 'Focussing on form in the classroom', *Occasional Papers*, Institute of Language Teaching and Learning: University of Auckland.

Emminghaus, W. B. (1987) 'Refugee adaptation: basic research issues and applications', in J. W. Berry and R. C. Annis (eds) *Ethnic Psychology: Research and Practice with Immigrants, Refugees, Native Peoples, Ethnic Groups and Sojourners* (pp. 53–68), Amsterdam: Swets and Zeitlinger.

Ennis, C. (1998) 'Preferential affect: the crux of the teacher expectancy issue', in J. Brophy (ed.) *Expectations in the Classroom* (Vol. 7, pp. 183–214), Greenwich, CT: JAI Press Inc.

Eslea, M. and Smith, P. K. (1998) 'The long term effectiveness of anti-bullying work in primary schools', *Educational Research*, 40: 203–18.

Fairbanks, C. M. (1992) 'Labels, literacy, and enabling learning: Glenn's story', *Harvard Educational Review*, 62: 475–93.

Fan, X. and Chen, M. (2001) 'Parental involvement and students' academic achievement: a meta-analysis', *Educational Psychology Review*, 13: 1–22.

Forness, S. R. (1981) 'Concepts of learning and behavior disorders: implications for research and practice', *Exceptional Children*, 48: 56–64.

Fox, M. (1995) 'Working to support refugee children in schools', in J. Trowell and M. Bower (eds) *The emotional needs of young children and their families*, London: Routledge.

Fox, P. G., Cowell, J. M. and Montgomery, A. C. (1994) 'The effects of violence on health and adjustment of Southeast Asian refugee children: an integrative review', *Public Health Nursing*, 11: 195–201.

Franson, C. (1996) '"Mainstreaming": issues and concerns', *TESOL in Context*, 6: 19–23.

Freeman, Y. and Freeman, D. (1999) 'School success for secondary English learners', in E. Franklin (ed.), *Reading and Writing in More than one Language: Lessons for Teachers* (pp. 1–28), Alexandria, VA: TESOL.

Freire, M. (1990) 'Refugees: ESL and literacy', *Refuge: Canada's Periodical on Refugees*, 10: 3–6.

Freitas, A. L. and Downey, G. (1998) 'Resilience: a dynamic perspective', *International Journal of Behavioural Development*, 22: 263–85.

Friedman, M. and Jaranson, J. (1994) 'The applicability of the posttraumatic stress disorder concept to refugees', in A. J. Marsella and T. Bornemann (eds) *Amidst Peril and Pain: The Mental Health and Well-Being of the World's Refugees*. (pp. 207–27), Washington, DC: American Psychological Association.

Fullan, M. G. (1994) 'Coordinating the top down and bottom up strategies for educational reform', in R. F. Elmore and S. H. Fuhrman (eds) *The Governance of Curriculum*, Alexandria, VA: ASCD.

Fullan, M. G. and Newton, E. E. (1988) 'School principals and change processes in the secondary school', *Canadian Journal of Education*. 13: 404–22.

Fullan, M. and Pomfret, A. (1977) 'Research on curriculum and instruction implementation', *Review of Educational Research*, 47: 335–97.

Fuller, B. and Clarke, P. (1994) 'Raising school effects while ignoring culture? Local conditions and the influence of classroom tools, rules and pedagogy', *Review of Educational Research*, 64: 119–57.

Fullilove, M. T. (1996) 'Psychiatric implications of displacement: contributions from the psychology of place', *American Journal of Psychiatry*, 153: 1516–23.

Further Education Unit, London (1994) (England) *Refugee Education and Training. Issues for Further Education*. ED383917.

Gardner, H. (1995) 'The development of competence in culturally defined domains: a preliminary framework', in N. R. Goldberger and J. B. Veroff (eds) *The Culture and Psychology Reader* (pp. 222–44), New York: New York University Press.

Garmezy, N. (1991) 'Resilience in children's adaptation to negative life events and stressed environments', *Pediatric Annals*, 20: 459–60, 463–6.

Gartner, A. and Lipsky, D. K. (1987) 'Inclusive schools' movement and the radicalisation of special education reform', *Exceptional Children*, 60: 294–309.

Gavrilidou, M., de Mesquita, P. B. and Mason, E. J. (1993) 'Greek teachers' judgments about the nature and severity of classroom problems', *School Psychology International*, 14: 169–80.

Gersten, R., Vaughn, S., Deshler, D. and Schiller, E. (1997) 'What we know about using research findings - implications for improving special education practice', *Journal of Learning Disabilities*, 30: 466–76.

Gibson, M. A. (1988) *Accommodation Without Assimilation: Sikh Immigrants in an American High School*, Ithaca, NY: Cornell University Press.

Glynn, T. and Glynn, V. (1986) 'Shared reading by Cambodian mothers and children learning English as a second language: reciprocal gains', *Exceptional Child*, 33: 159–72.

Good, T. and Weinstein, R. (1986) 'Schools make a difference: evidence, criticism, and new directions', *American Psychologist*, 41: 1090–7.

Gorney, D. J. and Ysseldyke, J. E. (1993) 'Students with disabilities use of various options to access alternative schools and area learning centers', *Special Services in the Schools*, 7: 125–43.

Grant, C. A. and Tate, W. F. (1995) 'Multicultural education through the lens of the multicultural education research literature', in J. A. Banks and C. A. M. Banks (eds) *Handbook of Research on Multicultural Education*, New York: Macmillan Publishing.

Gunderson, L. (2000) 'Voices of the teenage diasporas', *Journal of Adolescent and Adult Literacy*, 43: 692–706.

Gunderson, L. (2002) 'Reception classes for immigrant students in Vancouver', *TESOL Quarterly*, 36: 98–102.

Hahn, H. (1989) 'The politics of special education', in D. K. Lipsky and A. Gartner (eds) *Beyond Separate Education: Quality Education for All* (pp. 225–41), Baltimore, MD: Paul Brookes Publishing.

Hall, G. and Hord, S. (1987) *Change in Schools: Facilitating the Process*, New York: SUNY Press.

Hamilton, R., Frater-Mathieson, K., Moore, D., Anderson, A. and Loewen, S. (2001) *Kosova Project: Evaluation of Contexts, Input, Processes and Products*. Project funded by the Research and Statistics Division, Ministry of Education, Wellington, New Zealand.

Hargreaves, A. (1996) 'Transforming knowledge: blurring the boundaries between research, policy and practice', *Education Policy and Analysis*, 18: 105–22.

Harris, K. C. (1996) 'Collaboration within a multicultural society - issues for consideration', *Rase: Remedial and Special Education*, 17: 355–62.

Harvey, A. and Bryant, R. A. (1999) 'Dissociative symptoms in Active Stress Disorder', *Journal of Traumatic Stress*, 12: 673–9.

Henderson, A. E. (1987) *The Evidence Continues to Grow: Parental Involvement Improves Student Achievement*, Columbia, MD: National Committee for Citizens in Education.

Herman, J. (1992) *Trauma and Recovery*, USA: Basic Books.

Herman, J. (1993) 'Sequelae of prolonged and repeated trauma: evidence for a complex posttraumatic stress syndrome (DESNOS)', In J.R.T. Davidson and E.D. Foa (eds) *Post-traumatic Stress Disorder: DSM-IV and Beyond* (pp. 213–28), Washington, DC: American Psychiatric Press.

Hinton, R. (2000) 'Seen but not heard: refugee children and models for intervention', in Panter-Brick, C. and Smith, M. T. (eds) (2000) *Abandoned Children*. (pp. 199–212), New York: Cambridge University Press.

Hodes, M. (2000) 'Psychologically distressed refugee children in the United Kingdom', *Child Psychology and Psychiatry Review*, 5:57–68.

Hoyt, L. (1995) 'Enhancing the flavor: winning partnerships between home and schools', in D. Ranard and M. Pfleger (eds) *A Fifteen-year Experiment in Refugee Education*, ERIC Clearinghouse on Language and Linguistics.

Humpage, L. (1998) 'Cultural understanding: Somali students in Christchurch', *Many Voices*, 18: 8–10.

Humpage, L. (1999) 'Refugee or turmoil? Somali refugee adolescents in *Christchurch secondary schools*', Christchurch, NZ: A Report commissioned by Refugee Resettlement Support, Christchurch, New Zealand.

Hyder, T. (1998) 'Supporting refugee children in the early years', in C. Jones and J. Rutter (eds) *Refugee Education: Mapping the Field*, London: Trentham Books.

Hyman, I., Vu, N., and Beiser, M. (2000) 'Post-migration stresses among Southeast Asian refugee youth in Canada: a research note', *Journal of Comparative Family Studies*, 31: 281–93.

Ioup, G., Boustagui, E., El-Tigi, M. and Moselle, M. (1994) 'Re-examining the critical period hypothesis: a case study of successful adult SLA in a naturalistic environment', *Studies in Second Language Acquisition*, 16: 73–98.

Jansen, J. (1995) 'Effective schools?', *Comparative Education*, 31: 181–200.

Jones, C. (1998) 'The educational needs of refugee children', in C. Jones and J. Rutter (eds) *Refugee Education: Mapping the Field* (pp. 171–82), London: Trentham Books.

Jones, C. and Rutter, J. (1998) 'Mapping the field: current issues in refugee education.' In C. Jones and J. Rutter (eds) *Refugee Education: Mapping the Field*, London: Trentham Books.

Jupp, J. and Luckey, J. (1990) 'Educational experiences in Australia of Indo-Chinese adolescent refugees', *International Journal of Mental Health*, 18: 79–91.

Jussim, L., Smith, A., Madon, S. and Palumbo, P. (1998) 'Teacher expectations', in J. Brophy (ed.) *Expectations in the Classroom* (Vol. 7, pp. 1–48), Greenwich, CT: JAI Press Inc.

Kanal, B. and Adrienne, J. (1997) '"We came as refugees" – excerpts from Borany's story', *Many Voices: a Journal of New Settlers and Multicultural Education*, 11: 19–22.

Kaplan, I. (2000) *Guide to Working with Young People*, Australia: The Victorian Foundation for Survivors of Torture Inc.

Kaprielian-Churchill, I. (1996) 'Refugees and Education in Canadian Schools', *International Review of Education*, 42: 349–65.

Kaslow, N. J., Deering, C. G. and Racusin, G. R. (1994) 'Depressed children and their families', *Clinical Psychology Review*, 14: 39–59.

Kay, A. (1990) 'Teacher development and ESL in the mainstream', *TESOL in Context*, 1: 7–10.

Keith, T., Reimers, T., Fehrmann, P., Pottebaum, S. and Aubey, L. (1986) 'Parental involvement, homework, and TV time: direct and indirect effects on high school achievement', *Journal of Educational Psychology*, 78: 373–80.

Kelly, P. and Bennoun, R. (1984) *Students from Indo-China: Education issues: Resource Book*, Victoria: Australian Centre for Indo-Chinese Research.

Kennedy, S. and Dewar, S. (1997) *Non-English-Speaking Background Students: A Study of Programmes and Support in New Zealand Schools*, Wellington: Research Unit, Research and International Section, Ministry of Education.

Kinzie, J., Sack, W., Angell, R., Manson, S. and Rath, B. (1986) 'The psychiatric effects of massive trauma on Cambodian children', *Journal of the American Academy of Child Psychiatry*, 25: 377–83.

Krashen, S. (1982) *Principles and Practice in Second Language Acquisition*, Oxford: Pergamon.

Kube, D. A. and Shapiro, B. K. (1996) 'Persistent school dysfunction – unrecognized comorbidity and suboptimal therapy', *Clinical Pediatrics*, 35: 571–6.

Kuhn, T. S. (1970) *Structure of Scientific Revolutions* (2nd edn) (Vol. 2), Chicago: University of Chicago Press.

Landesman, S. and Ramey, C. (1989) 'Developmental psychology and mental retardation: Integrating scientific principles with treatment practices. Special issue:

children and their development: knowledge base, research agenda, and social policy application', *American Psychologist*, 44:409–15.

Lange, C. M., and Ysseldyke, J. E. (1994) 'Desired results of second chance programs', *Special Services in the Schools*, 9: 155–71.

Lange, C. M. and Ysseldyke, J. E. (1998) 'School choice policies and practices for students with disabilities', *Exceptional Children*, 64: 255–70.

Lee, V., Bryk, A. and Smith, J. (1993) 'The organisation of effective secondary schools', in L. Darling-Hammond (ed.) *Review of Research in Education* (Vol. 19, pp. 171–268), Washington, DC: American Educational Research Association.

Leiper de Monchy, M. (1991) 'Recovery and rebuilding: the challenge for refugee children and service providers', in F. Aheran and J. Athey (eds) *Refugee Children: Theory, Research, and Services*, Baltimore: The John Hopkins University Press.

Leung, C. (2001a) 'English as an additional language: distinct language focus or diffused curriculum concerns?', *Language and Education*, 15: 33–55.

Leung, C. (2001b) 'Evaluation of content-language learning in the mainstream classroom', in B. Mohan, C. Leung and C. Davison (eds) *English as a Second Language in the Mainstream: Teaching, Learning and Identity* (pp. 177–98), Harlow, England: Longman.

Leung, C. (2002) 'Reception classes for immigrant students in England', *TESOL Quarterly*, 36: 93–8.

Leung, C. and Franson, C. (2001) 'Mainstreaming: ESL as a diffused curriculum concern', in B. Mohan, C. Leung and C. Davison (eds) *English as a Second Language in the Mainstream: Teaching, Learning and Identity* (pp. 177–98), Harlow, England: Longman.

Lewis, M. (1997) *Journeys in Language Learning: ESOL Students in Elementary Classrooms Around the World*, Toronto: ITP Nelson.

Lewis, M. (1998) 'ESOL classes: to go or not to go?', *Many Voices*, 12: 4–7.

Lodge, C. (1998) 'Working with refugee children: one school's experience', in C. Jones and J. Rutter (eds) *Refugee Education: Mapping the Field*, London: Trentham Books.

Lopez, G., Scribner, J. and Mahitivanichcha, K. (2001) 'Redefining parental involvement: lessons from high-performing migrant-impacted schools', *American Educational Research Journal*, 38: 253–88.

Luthar, S. S., Doernberger, C. H. and Zigler, E. (1993) 'Resilience is not a unidimensional construct: insights from a prospective study of inner-city adolescents', *Development and Psychopathology*, 5: 703–17.

Luthar, S. S. and Zigler, E. (1991) 'Vulnerability and competence: a review of research on resilience in childhood', *American Journal of Orthopsychiatry*, 61: 6–22.

Masten, A. S., Best, K. M. and Garmezy, N. (1991) 'Resilience and development: contributions from the study of children who overcome adversity', *Development and Psychopathology*, 2:425–44.

Masten, A. S., and Coatsworth, J. D. (1998) 'The development of competence in favourable and unfavourable environments. Lessons from research on successful children', *American Psychologist*, 53: 205–20.

McCloskey, L. A. and Southwick, K. (1996) 'Psychosocial problems in refugee children exposed to war', *Pediatrics*, 97: 394–7.

McDonald, J. (1998) 'Refugee students' experiences of the UK educational system', in C. Jones and J. Rutter (eds) *Refugee Education: Mapping the Field* (pp. 149–70), London: Trentham Books.

McGoldrick, M., Pearce, J. and Giordano, J. (1986) *Ethnicity and Family Therapy*, IL: The Guildford Press.

McKelvey, R. S., Mao, A. R. and Webb, J. A. (1992) 'A risk profile predicting psychological distress in Vietnamese Amerasian youth', *Journal of the American Academy of Child and Adolescent Psychiatry*, 31: 911–15.

McLeskey, J. and Waldron, N. L. (1996) 'Responses to questions teachers and administrators frequently ask about inclusive school programs', *Phi Delta Kappan*, 78: 150–6.

Melzak, S. and Warner, R. (1992) *Integrating Refugee Children into Schools*, London: Medical Foundation/Minority Rights Group.

Meyen, E. L. (1995) 'A commentary on special education', in E. L. Meyen and T. M. Skrtic (eds) *Special Education and Student Disability* (4th edn), Denver, CO: Lane Publishing Company.

Mickelson, R. A. (1993) 'Minorities and education in plural societies', *Anthropology and Education Quarterly*, 24: 269–76.

Ministry of Education (1993) *The New Zealand Curriculum Framework*, Wellington: Learning Media.

Ministry of Education (1996) *Special Education 2000*, Wellington: Author.

Ministry of Education (1997) *Governing and Managing New Zealand Schools: A Guide for Boards of Trustees. Part One: The National Education Guidelines*, Wellington: Learning Media.

Miron, G. and Katoda, H. (1991) 'Education for persons with handicaps in Japan, the USA and Sweden', *Scandinavian Journal of Educational Research*, 35: 163–78.

Mohan, B., Leung, C. and Davison, C. (eds) (2001) *English as a Second Language in the Mainstream: Teaching, Learning and Identity*, Harlow, England: Longman.

Molman, G., Coladarci, T. and Gage, N. (1982) 'Comprehension and attitude as predictors of implementation of teacher training', *Journal of Teacher Education*, 33: 31–6.

Montgomery, E. (1998) 'Refugee children from the Middle East', *Scandinavian Journal of Social Medicine* (Suppl 54), 1–152.

Montgomery, E. (2000) 'European conference: empowerment of traumatised refugee families', *Torture*, 10: 20–1.

Montgomery, J. R. (1996) 'Components of refugee adaptation', *International Migration Review*, 3: 679–702.

Moore, D. W., Anderson, A., Timperley, H., Glynn, T., Macfarlane, A., Brown, D. and Thomson, C. (1999a) *Caught Between Stories: Special Education in New Zealand*, Literature Review Monograph Series. Wellington: New Zealand Council for Educational Research.

Neimeyer, R. (1998) *Lessons of Loss*, USA: Premis Customs Publishing.

Nelson, C. M. and Polsgrove, L. (1984) 'Behavior analysis in special education: white rabbit or white elephant?', *Rase: Remedial and Special Education*, 5: 6–17.

Nolin, M. (1996) 'Student victimization in school', *Journal of School Health*, 66: 216–21.

Nwadiora, E. and McAdoo, H. (1996) 'Acculturative stress among Amerasian refugees: gender and racial differences', *Adolescence*, 31: 477–87.

Ogbu, J. U. (1986) 'The consequences of the American caste systems', in U. Neisser (ed.) *The School Achievement of Minority Children: New Perspectives* (pp. 19–56), Hillsdale, NJ: Lawrence Erlbaum Associates.

Ogbu, J. U. (1988) 'Class stratification, racial stratification, and schooling', in L. Weiss (ed.) *Class, Race, and Gender in American Education* (pp. 163–82), Albany, NY: State University of New York Press.

Ogbu, J. U. (1995a) 'Cultural problems in minority education: their interpretations and consequences – part two: case studies', *The Urban Review*, 27: 271–97.

Ogbu, J. U. (1995b) 'Cultural problems in minority education: their interpretations and consequences-part one: theoretical background', *The Urban Review*, 27: 189–205.

Ogbu, J. U. (1995c) The origins of human competence: a cultural-ecological perspective', in J. B. Veroff (ed.) *The Culture and Psychology Reader* (pp. 245–75), New York: New York University Press.

Olweus, D. (1998) *Bullying at School: What we Know and What we Can Do*, Oxford: Blackwell.

Olweus, D. and Limber, S. (1999) 'Bullying prevention program', in D.S. Eliot (ed.) *Blueprint for Violence Prevention*, Denver, CO: C & M Press.

Osborne, S. S., Schulte, A. C. and McKinney, J. D. (1991) 'A longitudinal study of students with learning disabilities in mainstream and resource programs', *Exceptionality*, 2: 81–95.

Peirce, B. N. (1995) 'Social identity, investment, and language learning', *TESOL Quarterly*, 29: 9–31.

Pelligrini, A. D. (2002) 'Bullying, victimization, and sexual harassment during transition to middle school', *Educational Psychologist*, 37: 151–63.

Perreault, S. and Bourhis, R. Y. (1999) 'Ethnocentrism, social identification, and discrimination', *Personality and Social Psychology Bulletin*, 25: Jan 1999.

Perry, B. D. (1994) *The Effects of Traumatic Events on Children. Materials for parents*, (A CIVITAS Initiative Product), Houston, TX: Department of Psychiatry and behavioral Sciences, Baylor College of Medicine.

Peterson, R. and Ishii-Jordan, S. (eds) (1994) *Multicultural Issues in the Education for Students with Behavioural Disorders*, Cambridge, MA: Brookline Books.

Peterson, R., and Skiba, R. (2000) 'Creating school climates that prevent school violence', *Preventing School Failure*, 44: 122–30.

Pfefferbaum, B. (1997) 'Posttraumatic Stress Disorder in children - a review of the past 10 years', *Journal of the American Academy of Child and Adolescent Psychiatry*, 36: 1503–11.

Plummer, S. (1998) 'Treatment of traumatised children from various cultures', paper presented at the International Congress on Child Abuse and Neglect, Auckland, New Zealand.

Pollard, A. and Filer, A. (1996) *The Social World of Children's Learning: Case Studies from Four to Seven*, London: Cassell.

President's Commission on Excellence in Special Education (2002) *A New Era: Revitalising Special Education for Children and their Families*, U. S. Department of Education Office of Special Education and Rehabilitative Services, Washington DC.

Radke-Yarrow, M. and Brown, E. (1993) 'Resilience and vulnerability in children of multiple-risk families', *Development and Psychopathology*, 5: 581–92.

Rando, T. (1993) *Treatment of Complicated Mourning*, IL: Research Press.

Raywid, M. (1985) 'Family choice arrangements in public schools: a review of the literature', *Review of Educational Research*, 55: 435–67.

Ready, T. (1991) 'School and the passage of refugee youth from adolescence to adulthood', in F. Aheran and J. Athey (eds) *Refugee Children: Theory, Research, and Services*, Baltimore: The John Hopkins University Press.

Reichenberg, D. and Friedman, S. (1996) 'Healing the invisible wounds of children in war: a rights approach', in Y. Danieli, N. S. Rodley and L. Weisaeth (eds) *International Responses to Traumatic Stress: Humanitarian, Human Rights, Justice, Peace and Development Contributions, Collaborative Actions and Future Initiatives*, New York: Baywood Publishers.

Reynolds, D. and Teddlie, C. (2000) 'The processes of school effectiveness', in C. Teddlie and D. Reynolds (eds) *The International Handbook of School Effectiveness Research*, London: Falmer Press.

Reynolds, M. C. (1989) 'An historical perspective: the delivery of special education to mildly disabled and at-risk students', *Rase: Remedial and Special Education*, 10:7–11.

Reynolds, M. C. (1992) 'Students and programs at the school margins: disorder and needed repairs', *School Psychology Quarterly*, 7: 233–44.

Reynolds, M. C., Wang, M. C., and Walberg, H. J. (1987) 'The necessary restructuring of special and regular education', *Exceptional Children*, 53: 391–8.

Richman, N. (1998) *In the Midst of the Whirlwind: A Manual for Helping Refugee Children*, London: Trentham.

Roberts-Gray, C. (1985) 'Managing the implementation of innovations', *Evaluation and Program Planning*, 8: 261–9.

Roland, E. (2000) 'Bullying in school: three national innovations in Norwegian schools in 15 years', *Aggressive Behavior*, 26: 135–43.

Rosentholtz, S. (1989) *Teachers' Workplace: The Social Organisation of Schools*, New York: Longman.

Rousseau, C., Drapeau, A. and Corin, E. (1996) 'School performance and emotional problems in refugee children', *American Journal of Orthopsychiatry*, 66: 239–51.

Rousseau, C., Drapeau, A. and Corin, E. (1998) 'Risk and protective factors in Central American and Southeast Asian refugee children', *Journal of Refugee Studies*, 11: 20–37.

Ruma, P. R., Burke, R. V. and Thompson, R. W. (1996) 'Group parent training: is it effective for children of all ages?', *Behavior Therapy*, 27: 159–69.

Rutter, J. (1994) *Refugee Children in the Classroom*, London: Trentham.

Rutter, J. (1998) 'Refugees in today's world', in J. Rutter and C. Jones (eds) *Refugee Education: Mapping the Field* (pp. 13–32), London: Trentham

Rutter, J. and Hyder, T. (1998) *Refugee Children in the Early Years: Issues for Policy-makers and Providers*, London: Save the Children.

Samway, K. D. and Syvanen, C. (1999) 'Cross-age tutoring and ESOL students', in E. Franklin (ed.) *Reading and Writing in More than One Language: Lessons for Teachers* (pp. 49–64), Alexandria, VA: TESOL.

Sanders, M. G. and Epstein, J. L. (1998) 'International perspectives on School-Family-Community partnerships', *Childhood Education*, 74: 340–1

Sanmiguel, S. K., Forness, S. R. and Kavale, K. A. (1996) 'Social skills deficits in learning disabilities - the psychiatric comorbidity hypothesis', *Learning Disability Quarterly*, 19: 252–61.

Scheemers, J., Bosker, R. and Creemers, B. (2000) 'Time for self-criticism: on the viability of school effectiveness research', *School Effectiveness and School Improvement*, 12: 131–57.

Schlechty, P. and Vance, V. (1983) 'Recruitment, selection, and retention: the shape of the teaching force', *Elementary School Journal*, 83: 469–87.

Schmid, R. (1987) 'Historical perspectives of the ecological model', *Pointer*, 31: 5–8.

Schumann, J. H. (1986) 'Research on the acculturation model for second language acquisition', *Journal of Multilingual and Multicultural Development*, 7: 379–92.

Schumm, J. S. and Vaughn, S. (1995) 'Meaningful professional development in accommodating students with disabilities: lessons learned', *Rase: Remedial and Special Education*, 16: 344–52.

Sergiovanni, T. (1994) *Building Community in Schools*, San Francisco: Jossey-Bass.

Shalev, A.Y., Peri, T., Caneti, L. and Schreiber, S. (1996) 'Predictors of PTSD in injured trauma survivors', *American Journal of Psychiatry*, 53: 219–24.

Sherriff, J. E. (1995) *Reaching first base: Guidelines for Good Practice on Meeting the Needs of Refugee Children from the Horn of Africa*, London: Day-care Trust.

Silove, D., Tarn, R., Bowles, R. and Reid, J. (1991) 'Psychosocial needs of torture survivors', *Australian and New Zealand Journal of Psychiatry*, 25: 1–10.

Silverman, P. (2000) *Never Too Young to Know: Death in Children's Lives*, New York: Oxford University Press.

Sindelar, P. T. and Kilgore, K. L. (1995) 'Teacher education', in M. C. Wang, M. C. Reynolds, and H. J. Walberg (eds) *Handbook of Special and Remedial Education: Research and Practice* (pp. 393–432), Oxford: Pergamon.

Sizer, T. (1992) *Horace's School: Redesigning the American High School*, Boston, MA: Houghton Mifflin.

Skehan, P. (1989) *Individual Differences in Second-Language Learning*, London: Edward Arnold.

Skinner, K. A. and Hendricks, G. L. (1979) 'The shaping of ethnic self-identity among indochinese refugees', *The Journal of Ethnic Studies*, 7: 23–41.

Skrtic, T. M. (1995) 'The special education knowledge tradition: crisis and opportunity', in E. L. Meyen and T. M. Skrtic (eds) *Special Education and Student Disability* (4th edn), Denver, CO: Lane Publishing Company.

Sloper, T. and Tyler, S. (1992) 'Integration of children with severe learning difficulties in mainstream schools: evaluation of a pilot study', *Educational and Child Psychology*, 9: 34–45.

Smith, M. and Sheppard, L. (1988) 'Kindergarten readiness and retention: a qualitative study of teachers' beliefs and practices', *American Educational Research Journal*, 25: 307–33.

Snow, R., Corno, L. and Jackson III, D. (1996) 'Individual differences in affective and conative functions', in D. Berliner and R. Calfee (eds) *Handbook of Educational Psychology*, New York: Simon and Schuster Macmillan.

Sparks, L. (1989) *Anti-bias Curriculum: Tools for Empowering Young Children*, Washington, DC: National Association for the Education of Young Children.

Spitz, H. (1999) 'Beleaguered Pygmalion: a history of the controversy over claims that teacher expectancy raises intelligence', *Intelligence*, 27: 199–234.

Stainback, S. and Stainback, W. (1990) 'Inclusive schooling', in W. Stainback and S. Stainback (eds) *Support Networks for Inclusive Schooling*, Baltimore: Paul Brookes Publishing.

Staudacher, C. (1987) *Beyond Grief*, USA: New Harbinger Publications.

Stead, J., Closs, A. and Arshad, R. (1999) *Refugee Pupils in Scottish Schools, Spotlight*, Edinburgh, Scotland: Scottish Council for Research in Education.

Stoehr, M. (2001) 'Danish article on psychoeducation with Kosovo Albanian refugee children', *Torture*, 11: 123.

Stringfield, S. and Herman, R. (1996) 'Assessment of the state for school effectiveness research in the United States of America', *School Effectiveness and School Improvement*, 7:159–80.

Swain, M. (1985) 'Communicative competence: some roles of comprehensible input and comprehensible output in its development', in C. Madden (ed.) *Input in Second Language Acquisition*, Rowley, MA: Newbury House.

Swain, M. (1995) 'Three functions of output in second language learning', in G. Cook and B. Seidlhofer (ed.) *For H. G. Widdowson: Principles and Practice in the Study of Language*, Oxford: Oxford University Press.

Taleni, T. (1998) 'Newly migrated Samoan students in New Zealand schools', *Many Voices*, 12: 21–8.

Tavener, J. and Glynn, T. (1989) 'Peer tutoring of reading as a context for learning English as a second language', *Language and Reading: An International Journal*, 3: 1–11.

Teddlie, C. and Reynolds, D. (2000) 'Countering the critics: responses to recent criticisms of school effectiveness research', *School Effectiveness and School Improvement*, 12: 41–82.

Teddlie, C. and Stringfield, S. (1993) *Schools Make a Difference: Lessons Learned From a 10-year Study of School Effects*, New York: Teachers College.

Terr, L. (1991) 'Childhood traumas: an outline and overview', *American Journal of Psychiatry*, 148: 10–20.

Thomson, C. (1998, July) 'Inclusion in the professional development of resource teachers learning and behaviour', paper presented at the Australian Teacher Education Association 28th Annual Conference, Melbourne, Australia.

Timperley, H. S. and Robinson, V. M. J. (1997) 'The problem of policy inplementation: the case of performance appraisal', *School Leadership and Management*, 17: 333–45.

Trump, L. (1990) 'The school psychologist as action researcher: fostering developments in one special school', *School Psychology International*, 11:187–93.

Udvari-Solnar, A. (1994) 'A decision making model for curricular adaptation in cooperative groups', in J. S. Thousand, R. A. Villa and A. I. Nevin (eds) *Creativity and Collaborative Learning: A Practical Guide to Empowering Students and Teachers* (pp. 59–77), Baltimore: Paul Brooks.

Udvari-Solnar, A. (1995) 'Designing effective adaptations for inclusive classrooms', *Network*, 4: 31–5.

United Nations High Commission for Refugees (1993) The 1951 Refugee Convention: Questions and Answers. http://www.unhcr.ch.

United Nations High Commission for Refugees (2002) Basic Facts. http://www.unhcr.ch.

Van der Veer, G. (1998) *Counselling and Therapy with Refugees and Victims of Trauma*, New York: John Wiley and Sons.

Van der Veer, G. (2000) 'Empowerment of traumatised refugees: a developmental approach to prevention and treatment', *Torture*, 10:8–11.

van Hees, J. (1994) *A Guideline for Primary School: Effective Provisions for Students from Language Backgrounds Other than English*, Auckland: Education Advisory Services, Auckland College of Education.

van Hees, J. (1997) 'Assisting students from non-English speaking backgrounds: some questions primary school teachers frequently ask', *Many Voices: A Journal of New Settlers and Multicultural Education*, 10: 4–9.

Vantilburg, M. A. L., Vingerhoets, A. and Vanheck, G. L. (1996) 'Homesickness - a review of the literature', *Psychological Medicine*, 26: 899–912.

Vaughn, S., Hughes, M. T., Schumm, J. S. and Klingner, J. (1998) 'A collaborative effort to enhance reading and writing instruction in inclusion classrooms', *Learning Disability Quarterly*, 21:57–74.

Wagner, P. and Lodge, C. (1995) *Refugee Children in School*: National Association of Pastoral Care in Education. NAPCE Dept. of Education, University of Warwick.

Waite, J. (1992) *Aotearoa: Speaking for Ourselves: A Discussion on the Development of a New Zealand Languages Policy*, Wellington: Learning Media for the Ministry of Education.

Waldegrave, C. (1993) 'Just Therapy', *Dulwich Centre Newsletter*, 1, 6–46.

Walker, J., Moore, D. W., Anderson, A., Brown, D., Thomson, L., Glynn, T. and Macfarlane, A. (1999) 'Innovative inclusion initiative: the resource teachers in learning and behaviour program', paper presented at The Joint Conference of Australian Association for Research in Education and New Zealand Association for Research in Education, Melbourne, Australia.

Wang, M. C., Reynolds, M. C. and Walberg, H. J. (1991) 'Integrating second-system children: alternatives to segregation and classification of handicapped children', in R. Constable, J. P. Flynn and S. McDonald (eds) *School Social Work: Practice and Research Perspectives* (pp. 156–1660), Chicago: Lyceum Books.

Wassef, A., Mason, G., Collins, M.-L., O'Boyle, M. and Ingham, D. (1996) 'In search of effective programs to address students' emotional distress and behavioral problems part III: student assessment of school-based support groups', *Adolescence*, 31: 1–16.

Watts, N., White, C. and Trlin, A. (2001) *English Language Provision for Adult Immigrants and/or Refugees from non-English Speaking Backgrounds in Educational Institutions and Training Establishments in New Zealand*, Palmerston North, New Zealand: New Settlers Programme, Massey University.

Waugh, R. (1994) 'Teachers' receptivity to system-wide change in a centralised education system', *Education, Research and Perspectives*, 21: 80–94,

Waugh, R. and Godfrey, J. (1995) 'Understanding teacher's receptivity to system-wide educational change', *Journal of Educational Administration*, 33: 38–54.

Waugh, R. and Punch, K. (1987) 'Teacher receptivity to system-wide change in the implementation stage', *Review of Educational Research*, 57: 237–55.

Waxman, H. and Walberg, H. (1991) *Effective Teaching: Current Research*, Berkeley: McCutchen.

Wehby, J. H., Symons, F. J. and Hollo, A. (1997) 'Promote appropriate assessment', *Journal of Emotional and Behavioral Disorders*, 5: 45–54.

Weinstein, R. and McKown, C. (1998) 'Expectancy effects in context', in J. Brophy (ed.) *Expectations in the Classroom* (Vol. 7, pp. 215–42), Greenwich, CT: JAI Press Inc.

Werner, E. E. (1993) 'Risk, resilience, and recovery: perspectives from the Kauai Longitudinal Study', *Development and Psychopathology*, 5: 503–15.

Werner, E. E., Randolph, S. M., and Masten, A. S. (29 March 1996) 'Fostering resilience in kids: overcoming adversity', paper presented at the Congressional Breakfast Seminar, 2168 Rayburn House Office Building.

Westermeyer, J. and Her, C. (1996) 'Predictors of English fluency among Hmong refugees in Minnesota: a longitudinal study', *Cultural Diversity and Mental Health*, 2: 125–32.

Will, M. (1988) 'Educating students with learning problems and the changing role of the school psychologist', *School Psychology Review*, 17: 476–8.

Willems, E. P. (1973) 'Behavioral ecology and experimental analysis: courtship is not enough', in J. R. Nesselroade and H. W. Reese (eds) *Life-Span Developmental Psychology: Methodological Issues* (pp. 79–110), New York: Academic Press.

Wilson, M. S. (1991) 'Support services professionals' evaluation of current services for students with learning disabilities and low achieving students without learning disabilities: more grist for the reform mill', *School Psychology Review*, 20: 67–80.

Witmer, T. A. P. and Culver, S. M. (2001) 'Trauma and resilience among Bosnian refugee families: a critical review of the literature', *Journal of Social Work Research and Evaluation*, 2: 173–87.

York, J. and Tundidor, M. (1995) 'Issues raised in the name of inclusion: perspectives of educators, parents, and students', *Journal of the Association for Persons with Severe Handicaps*, 20: 31–44.

Ysseldyke, J. E. and Christenson, S. L. (1987) 'Evaluating students' instructional environments. Special Issue: Special education program evaluation', *Rase: Remedial and Special Education*, 8: 17–24.

Ysseldyke, J. E. and Christenson, S. L. (1993) *TIES II: The Instructional Environment System – II*. (4th edn), Longmont, CO: Sopris West.

Zhou, M. and Bankston, C. III (2000) *Straddling Two Social Worlds: The Experience of Vietnamese Refugee Children in the US*, ERIC Clearinghouse on Urban Education.

Index